"EVERYTHING YOU'VE HEARD ABOUT GEORGE STEINBRENNER IS TRUE. THAT'S THE PROBLEM."
—Dave Winfield

"A LIAR . . . A TYRANT . . . A GRACELESS LOUT . . . A STATESMAN IN THE ALEXANDER HAIG MOLD."
—Mike Lupica,
Daily News columnist

"AN UNREGISTERED EGOMANIAC AND ALL-TIME SECOND GUESSER."
—Ray Fitzgerald,
Boston Herald columnist

"THE MORE WE LOSE, THE MORE OFTEN STEINBRENNER WILL FLY IN. AND THE MORE HE FLIES, THE BETTER THE CHANCE THERE WILL BE OF THE PLANE CRASHING."
—Graig Nettles,
Yankee third baseman

"HE SHOULD REALLY STICK TO HORSES. AT LEAST HE CAN SHOOT THEM WHEN THEY SPIT THE BIT."
—Reggie Jackson,
Yankee outfielder and Hall-of-Famer

"HE'S LIKE A *TITANIC* IN SEARCH OF AN ICEBERG."
—Bowie Kuhn,
former Baseball Commissioner

Hey, let's be fair to George, just as fair as he is to everyone who crosses his path or gets in his way. After all, who would want to knife the Peerless Leader in the back when he's so good at doing it to himself . . . ?

◆

THE WIT AND WISDOM OF
George Steinbrenner

THE

WIT AND WISDOM

OF

GEORGE
STEINBRENNER

◆

FRANK COFFEY

Introduction by
PETER GOLENBOCK

Ⓢ

A SIGNET BOOK

SIGNET
Published by the Penguin Group
Penguin Books USA Inc., 375 Hudson Street,
New York, New York 10014, U.S.A.
Penguin Books Ltd., 27 Wrights Lane,
London W8 5TZ, England
Penguin Books Australia Ltd, Ringwood,
Victoria, Australia
Penguin Books Canada Ltd, 10 Alcorn Avenue,
Toronto, Ontario, Canada M4V 3B2
Penguin Books (N.Z.) Ltd, 182–190 Wairau Road,
Auckland 10, New Zealand

Penguin Books Ltd, Registered Offices:
Harmondsworth, Middlesex, England

First published by Signet, an imprint of New American Library,
a division of Penguin Books USA Inc.

First Printing, April, 1993
10 9 8 7 6 5 4 3 2 1

◆

THIS BOOK IS FOR
JOHN PALMER,
WHO LAUGHED EARLY
AND OFTEN.

◆

Contents

◆

Acknowledgments

◆

The author would like, first, to thank John Pynchon Holms, whose thorough research and acerbic wit were invaluable. Art Brennan, friend with jump shot, provided warm support on some cold days. My brother, Wayne Coffey, wielded a deft editorial pen, as did Bronx humorist and shanakee extraordinaire, Pat Kennedy. Aleks Rozens's research was invaluable and much appreciated. Thanks also to agent/co-conspirator Tony Seidl, adroit editors Michaela Hamilton and Danielle Perez and New American Library's fiercely brilliant art director George Cornell. And to all those talented and tenacious writers and reporters who heard and recorded the Boss's bon mots up close and personal . . . better you than me.

◆

"I wasn't any good at baseball. I never played it."

—George Steinbrenner

◆

Introduction

◆

Frank Coffey and I go way back. We met at Prentice-Hall, where he edited *Dynasty: The New York Yankees 1949–64*, my first book. The year was 1973, a watershed year in New York Yankees history. Mike Burke, Gabe Paul, and a third guy, from Cleveland of all places, were buying the Yankees from the Columbia Broadcasting System.

Frank and I both applauded the sale. CBS had bought an empty shell of a team from Dan Topping and Del Webb, the architects of the Dynasty years. True, the CBS Yankees had become respectable by 1972, but the team on the field was still a boring, pedestrian group. We loved that CBS would do things like having poet Marianne Moore throw out the first ball, but for fans used to rooting for stars, *big* stars, year after year, the cast of Roy White, Horace Clark, Gene Michael, Cereino Sanchez, Ron Blomberg, and Bobby Murcer didn't give a Yankee fan much of an adrenaline rush.

This was the milieu into which Burke, Gabe, and the Third Guy from Cleveland arrived. Mike Burke, who once was a spy for the OSS and the head of Ringling Brothers, thought he was going to run the team. But Burke was a gentleman, and he wasn't prepared for the Palace Coup.

Early in that first season Mike Burke was gone, drummed out of town by the Third Guy from Cleveland, whose name was George Steinbrenner.

Shortly thereafter, the staid, humdrum days fled. Catfish Hunter, and then Andy Messersmith, and Pat Dobson came to the Yankees, magically. The Third Guy was doing what Ed Barrow and George Weiss had done before, bought star players from other teams. Hunter had been a free agent on a fluke, but this man Steinbrenner paid more cash than any other team, and we Yankee fans were given the gift of being allowed to root for the mustachioed Mr. Hunter.

The effervescent Billy Martin replaced the dull Bill Virdon. Under Martin, the protégé of the great Casey Stengel, the architect of the Dynasty years, the Yankees won the pennant in 1976. Frank Coffey and I and the other Yankee fans couldn't believe our good fortune.

The next year the greatest slugger of the generation, Reggie Jackson, was added to the line-up. In 1977 and 1978, there were world championships and terrible turmoil. We overlooked the turmoil because of the championships. We didn't realize that the turmoil would be the constant.

Except for a fluke opportunity to be in the playoffs in 1981 because of the players' strike, the Yankee cupboard has remained bare since that magical year of 1978, when the Yankees came from fourteen games back to catch the Boston Red Sox and win the pennant on Bucky Dent's miraculous home run. The Series win over the Los Angeles Dodgers was a given.

And then the Reign of Terror started. There were firings. Every year, sometimes twice a year. In 1982 the Yankees had three managers and five pitching coaches. Managers were swapped around like chips at a poker game.

Along with the uncertainty of who would lead came constant criticism and shuffling of Yankee ball players. One rookie pitcher was "gutless," another was said to "spit the bit." Players were excoriated by the owner in the papers—the bigger the star, the greater the criticism. Billy Martin, Reggie Jackson, and Dave Winfield were the underlings in the news most often. All were derided and sent packing before their time.

By 1982 there were no stars left on the team. There was only one media celebrity: the owner.

And a funny thing happened. Yankee fans no longer enjoyed rooting for the Yankees. They had been squeezed out of it like Scrooge at Christmas.

We desperately needed another outlet. Fortunately, a lot of us discovered Rotisserie Baseball, and so rather than root for the New York Mets or another American League team, we were able to love the Yankees as a member of a dysfunctional family would love his own family—from afar—suffering along with the Yankee players who were abused and misused, and at the same time root for our individual Rotisseries players during the season.

The suffering continues. How could it be that the Yankees haven't been a force for fifteen years? And could it be that as long as George Steinbrenner owns the Yankees, this team, once the pride of the American League, will never win again? Yes, it is very possible.

And so Frank Coffey and I through the years have shared a great deal—our love for the Yankees of Casey Stengel—Mickey Mantle, Whitey Ford, Yogi Berra, and Roger Maris—and our love for the Yankees of Billy Martin—Reggie Jackson, Thurman Munson, and Lou Piniella.

We also share a deep longing, and a sad frustration, common to millions of Yankee fans, in that our once proud team has been taken from us by a man who has purloined it for his personal pleasure. It's no longer the New York Yankees, but rather the New York Steinbrenner.

He's silver-tongued George, partly truth and partly fiction. There has never been another sports owner like him. In this book Frank Coffey will let George tell you all about himself.

—Peter Golenbock

Author's Foreword

◆

We're not making this up: George Steinbrenner was born in a town called Rocky Road. As metaphor for The Boss's life, it is, if not perfect, damned good.

Perhaps George's road is better characterized as boulder-strewn. Ask Yogi Berra, an authentic Yankee hero, whose firing has been for me the lowest point of Steinbrenner's twenty-year series of dead-low tides. So far.

Others have their own nadir-of-the-month choices. A friend of mine who grew up in upstate Rochester, New York, ear glued to a crystal radio set as he meticulously filled scorebook after scorebook, cites the public apology after the 1981 World Series loss as the day he took off his Yankee cap and jacket. He hasn't put them on again, hasn't seen or heard or watched a Yankee game in twelve years. And believe me, Mike Seitzinger was a hopeless Yankee nut case. An embarrassment. The kind of fan every team should have.

The Dodger apology (If you don't win, you're a loser. Is there a philosophy more self-defeating?), though popular, has competition. How about humiliating Reggie Jackson by ordering a mid-season physical when the slugger was in a slump? (The suspicion, of course, was that Steinbrenner was trying to ruin Jackson's market value—the damaged goods ploy—in order to financially wound the soon-to-be free agent). Or the soap opera with an overmatched Billy Martin.

There are so many choices. Dave Winfield. Howie Spira. Fay Vincent. Toying with proud Lou Piniella, whom he often called a surrogate son, and firing him twice. Dumping Bucky Dent in Boston? (The site of, arguably, the greatest Yankee moment of them all— Dent's playoff home run.) Not an earth-shattering profanity, but simply mean and small.

And there's the non-public stuff perpetrated on those who couldn't fight back—secretaries, assistants, drivers, his "baseball people"—people who needed their jobs, who had to take the abuse. Writer Dick Schaap once characterized the way The Boss yells at employees "as just cruel."

This lifelong fan feels about the Yankees as Jack Nicholson in the film *Easy Rider* did about America: "You know, this used to be a helluva good country. . . . I can't understand what happened to it."

But we shouldn't forget there were high points, wondrous ones. Chris Chambliss's ninth-inning home run in 1976 to win the Yankees thirtieth pennant, and first since 1964, the last year of the Dynasty's years. Reggie's three taters against the Dodgers in the 1977 World Series. The 1978 return from the grave, when the Yankees, fourteen games back in July, staged baseball's greatest comeback to take the pennant. Thurman Munson's eighth-inning home run in game three of the '78 playoffs, offsetting the magnificent George Brett's three home runs.

And then there was the night of July 30, 1990, when it was announced to fans at Yankee Stadium that George Steinbrenner had been put on the permanently ineligible list, and the crowd stood and cheered for ninety seconds. That was good.

Better still was Reggie Jackson's first game back after leaving the Yankees. It was a dark and stormy night—I know, I was there—April 27, 1982. Bob Lemon had been sacked for the second time the day before. Ron Guidry was on the mound. In his first at-bat Jackson crushed a home run, the ball banging against the three-deck facade and bouncing back onto the wet field like an unexploded grenade. The explosion came momentarily, when the crowd erupted with a spontaneous chant: "Steinbrenner Sucks! Steinbrenner Sucks!" The owner, in attendance in his box, was not amused. I was. So was Guidry, who, as the sing-along echoed through the stadium, hid a grin behind his glove. Later he said, "It was the only fun I had out there."

Since Jackson's departure—coincidentally?—George Steinbrenner's Yankees have been losers. The post-season bleakness is eleven years and counting, tying the longest drought in the team's history (1965–75), for which Steinbrenner can also claim partial credit. In response, fans banded together in organizations like SOS (Stamp Out Steinbrenner) and BOSS (Battered Onlookers Sick of Steinbrenner); others produced protest T-shirts of which BOSS BUSTERS is a personal favorite. All for naught: The Boss, like poison ivy, is back. O Joy!

The Wit & Wisdom of George Steinbrenner is silly, not meant to be taken seriously by anyone. Including George. But let's face it, a sense of humor has not been one of the Principal Owner's defining characteristics. So there's the tiniest chance the parody, satire, and irony herein contained may annoy our Bossness. (He's good at annoyed.) Ah, well—the price of fame.

And, let's be perfectly clear: George Steinbrenner is not evil. His acts of private and public charity, invariably cited by friends, are legendary. And laudable.

However, here we're focusing on laughable. There's plenty of material. A lot of it is just plain odd. But *Wit & Wisdom* is all in good, clean American fun. Honest.

Speaking of odd: In 1981, *Playgirl* magazine named George M. Steinbrenner III one of "The Ten Sexiest Men in America." What were they thinking?

George on Modern
Employee Relations

*"You know I never second-guess
my people."*

◆ AND EXECUTED AT DAWN

"If he doesn't call me back in five minutes, he's fired."

—about Bill Kane, the Yankees' traveling secretary (1980)

◆ GO TO THE BANK ON THIS ONE

"I pay the bills around here. I'll say whatever I want." (1978)

◆ WHERE DO WE SIGN UP?

"Sometimes—as much as I don't want to—I have to inflict pain. But I also *inflict* some joy."

—explaining his complex carrot-and-stick management philosophy (1977)

◆ BUT THE INFLICTED JOY MAKES IT ALL WORTHWHILE

"I know I'm not easy to work for." (1977)

◆ WHERE'S MR. ED NOW THAT WE REALLY NEED HIM?

"Horses are great. They never complain, and they can't talk to sportswriters and tell them what a bum the owner is." (1980)

◆ FROM THE LIPS OF A BIG-TIME LOYALTY GUY

"I'm disappointed. Not in losing the arbitration, but in the young man. I don't think he showed much loyalty."

—on losing Rick Cerone's arbitration case in 1981

◆ A POIGNANT COMMENTARY ON THE DIRE CONDITION OF THE FLORIDA ECONOMY

"Boy, I really let her have it, called her some of the nastiest things. I told her I never wanted to see her again."

—remembering an incident with a secretary—who remained on the job (1987)

◆ GUILT IS A MANY-SPLENDORED THING

"I called one of my guys and asked about her kids. I said, 'She's got a young kid going to college, doesn't she? We'll pay for it.' Sometimes I react spontaneously like that."

—following up his firing with beneficence. In the interest of fair play it should be noted that the secretary, knowing the drill, showed up the next day to work and kept her job.

◆ CLYDE GOETH BEFORE A FALL

"What the hell was he doing at home? He's supposed to be scouting."

—when informed that 63-year-old Clyde King had fallen out of a treehouse and suffered a fractured collarbone and other injuries (1989)

◆ PLUS WE GOT SANDWICHES, AND ICE CREAM AND CRACKER JACKS, AND WE'LL JUST HAVE THE BEST TIME EVER!

"Why would you want to stay manager and be second-guessed by me when you can come up into the front office and be one of the second-guessers?"

—to a disappointed Gene Michael after his firing as manager in 1981

◆ AND THE SOUND YOU HEAR IN THE BACKGROUND IS A CHORUS OF CEO'S SINGING, "WE SHALL OVERCOME."

"I don't know about you boys, but I'll be eating three meals a day."

—said, according to the Washington Post, in negotiations with union leaders at the Steinbrenner-owned American Ship Building plant in Lorain, Ohio, 1983. The 87-year-old facility was closed a few weeks before Christmas with the loss of 1,500 jobs.

◆ WE DON'T DOO-DAH ANYMORE

"We ought to get a guy over there who can strut like that guy in Detroit. We can't overdo it. We got to have a guy who looks spontaneous. But we need a strutter, the old darktown shuffle."

—on hiring groundskeepers who can both entertain and rake (1977)

◆ PASS THE SLEDGE

"There's an image about me, which doesn't bother me. I don't consider being called The Boss in New York a negative. People naturally don't like their boss. But I'd rather be The Boss than The Wimp. I'd rather be the hammer than the nail. That's what I'm saying."

—discussing the low opinion many New Yorkers inexplicably seem to hold about him (1987)

◆ KEELHAULING IS ALSO AN OPTION

"I just don't know what my people are doing or what they're thinking. If they let him go, they ought to be shot."

—commenting about the long delay in signing Yankee first-round draft choice, left-handed pitcher Brien Taylor (1991)

◆ MY WILDEST DREAMS USUALLY INVOLVE KATE SMITH, A DWARF, SOME WHIP CREAM AND . . . WELL, NEVER MIND

"Never in my wildest dreams would I have paid that kid a million and a half. My understanding from reading the papers was [the Yankees offered] $650,000. I never dealt with numbers. I never talked numbers. I said I'd love to see them sign their first-round draft choice. I never said, 'Go spend a million and a half.' On a high school kid? No way."

—angry that the Yankee front office signed Brien Taylor to an expensive contract. Fay Vincent later held Steinbrenner's own comments—comparing Taylor to Dwight Gooden and Roger Clemens—"partially responsible" for the size of the contract. (August 1991)

◆ LIFE IMITATING ART?

"Where is it written that if you don't get results right away, you fire somebody? . . . Only a jackass would do that."

> —in a self-parodying skit on Saturday Night Live, Oct. 20, 1990. That same night—a moment of supreme irony—the Cincinnati Reds, managed by Lou Piniella, whom he fired twice, won the World Series in a four-game sweep.

◆ YOU CAN CATCH MORE FLIES WITH HUNS

"Huns learn much faster when faced with adversity."

> —discussing a metaphorical book titled "Leadership Secrets of Attila the Hun" (1990)

◆ WENT THROUGH A WHOLE BOX OF CRAYONS

"It's an excellent book. I've read it over and over. My copy in my office in Florida is all marked up."

> —about "Leadership Secrets of Attila the Hun" (1990)

◆ SELL THIS GUY A BRIDGE

"You know I wondered if this Attila the Hun was for real, or comical. But I think it's real, or close to it."

> —about "Leadership Secrets of Attila the Hun" (1990)

◆ PILLAGING AND PLUNDERING IN THE DEFENSE OF LIBERTY IS NO VICE

"Well, he wasn't perfect, but he did have some good things to say."

—about Attila the Hun

◆ AND THE ROSS PEROT REALITY AWARD GOES TO . . .

"No. I was often misquoted. I was supportive of my managers, even though they all may not think so."

—answering the question: Did you ever undermine your managers in the press? (1991)

◆ HERE AT YANKEE STADIUM WE PRIDE OURSELVES ON CREATING A STRESS-FREE ENVIRONMENT

"It better be done by the start of the season because you can't have this stuff weighing on the guy."

—on the arbitration of the Winfield foundation dispute (1988)

◆ BULLY FOR YOU

"Here I've got a strength coach who can't keep my players from getting hurt, and then I've got this asshole who can't get 'em healthy again."

—about Yankee strength coach Jeff Mangold and longtime trainer Gene Monahan. The remarks were made during an injury-riddled 1986 season.

◆ AND KEEP YOUR HANDS OFF THE OFFICE SUPPLIES BECAUSE WE'LL BE CHECKING ALL BAGS ON THE WAY OUT

"Clear out your desk, you're through."

> —firing a no-doubt deserving employee
> (1978)

◆ AND DON'T EVEN THINK ABOUT TAKING THOSE RUBBER BANDS

"Look, I'm going to miss a meeting because you screwed up. Just pack up your stuff."

> —how he fired a secretary from an airport
> phone because she failed to confirm a
> plane reservation (1990)

◆ ESPECIALLY IF I'M IN AN ELEVATOR

"I know I'm tough, but I try to make it up to my people in other ways. I don't like to hurt people. Sometimes I just . . . well, I guess I can't help it."

> —introspection, in and of itself, is painful
> (1978)

◆ ERRR . . . BOSS, THAT MIGHT MAKE IT A LITTLE HARD TO ROLL OUT OF THE WAY

"I know, let's let the air out of his tires."

> —mad that an employee's car was
> blocking Donald Trump's Lincoln after a
> spring training game in 1986

◆ MR. SYMPATHY

"It's the man's personal business. There are no extenuating circumstances. The man is being paid $1.1 million to play baseball. If you or I had a job somewhere and didn't show up and didn't call the boss, you wouldn't be working tomorrow. It's the same with a businessman or a man driving a cab. Let the punishment fit the crime. He can do his apologizing to his teammates who he let down."

> —about Ken Griffey, who missed a game
> due to a "major family problem"—i.e., a
> marital dispute. Griffey was fined
> $10,000—about two games salary.
> (June 1986)

◆ FROM THE JOURNALS OF DOCTOR FRANKENSTEINBRENNER

"I'm just trying to make a better man out of Nettles."

> —commenting on the human potential
> movement . . . no, wait, that's wrong.
> Commenting on a contract dispute with his
> star third baseman in which he forced
> Nettles to back down (1977)

◆ GEEZ, IT WAS A SUGGESTION, GUYS. IT JUST SOUNDED LIKE AN ORDER

"If you are willing to undertake this dedication, I want to know. If you feel you are unable to comply, or not interested, or would rather be part of another organization, I will do my best to place you any- where you might be happy. . . . I am hopeful that will not be the case."

> —from a letter to each of the Yankee players "requesting" that they volunteer for early spring training in 1982. The request was seen by many as a threat, and the Players Association and various concerned civil libertarians got involved— but many of the players caved in. Despite the huge advantage of early spring training, the Yankees finished fifth.

◆ A LIFE UNEXAMINED IS A LIFE NOT WORTH LIVING

"I guess I am a son of a bitch to work for." (August 1990)

POP QUIZ

Read the paragraph below and the two quotations following, then choose the quotation you believe comes closest
to being true. Mark your answer in the box provided with
a Number 2 Yankee lead pencil.

> After the 1980 season ended, George Stein-
> brenner offered the job of third-base coach to
> Don Zimmer without informing the team's man-
> ager, Dick Howser.

1. "George still hasn't talked about it, but I would think I
should be given the courtesy of approving or disapproving
the coaches that are added to the ball club. You know, I
have to work with these guys every day. Certainly as manager I should be able to say who's going to coach and
who's not going to coach."

2. "I don't appreciate Dick Howser popping off like this.
Howser I can't figure out. I'm very upset. I'm very disappointed in him. My staff is in agreement with everything I
have projected, and we're not quite ready to have Dick
Howser start running the New York Yankees totally yet."

Partly Truth, Partly Fiction

"I keep saying it and people say they don't believe it but it's true."

◆ CHECK YOUR BOOTS FOR COWPIE, PARDNER

"A lot of times making someone a consultant is putting him out to pasture or a settlement. This isn't the case here."

> —about Mike Burke, who three months
> after buying the team with Steinbrenner
> was being forced out as Yankee president.
> For all intents and purposes, Burke's
> participation with the Yankees ended that
> April of 1973.

◆ EAT MY DUST, PINOCCHIO

"It will never happen again."

> —on covering up, through misinformation,
> a serious injury to Yankee shortstop
> Mickey Klutts that would have ensured the
> team would have paid more dearly for
> White Sox shortstop Bucky Dent (1977)

◆ A VOICE IN THE WILDERNESS

"I know you don't believe it, nobody does, but it's true."

> —on his promise that team president Al
> Rosen would have total control of the
> team (1979)

22

◆ THE-BOSS-WHO-CRIED-WOLF

"I can't say anything bad about Billy, because I really like the guy. I keep saying it and people say they don't believe it but it's true. I care about him. I do." (1983)

◆ WHICH IS WHY GOD CREATED LAWYERS

"[I've made] statements that I believed were true when I made them."

—commenting on his testimony before baseball commissioner Fay Vincent in the Howie Spira case (August 6, 1990)

◆ REACH OUT AND CLUTCH SOMEONE

"I never called a manager in the dugout to dictate who should play or to say that he'd made a mistake."

—answering an interviewer's question about reports of interfering with managers during games (1991)

◆ SO ABOUT THE STUFF YOU TOLD US BEFORE . . .

"That was the commissioner's feeling. And I have been so consumed with the Olympic games and the United States Olympic team and the Olympic Committee that I really am not even—have not even met with the people who have been representing me with the commissioner. And I can say that honestly."

—answering Larry King's question about the date of his reinstatement to baseball (1992)

◆ WE'RE NOT EATING IT

"I don't like to talk about firing managers. I'm shifting people in everyone's interest: Billy's, Yogi's, mine."

—firing Martin, hiring Berra (December 1983)

◆ SURE FEELS LIKE SOMEBODY'S BEEN CANNED

"You can choose to look at it that way, but I'm shifting personnel. Nobody's been fired."

—Martin, Berra redux

GEORGE ON GEORGE

"Some guys can lead through genuine respect. . . . I'm not that kind of leader."

——————

◆ A SCARY THOUGHT

"I've mellowed some." (1980)

◆ BUT I'M A NICE PERSON, AND THAT'S WHAT IS REALLY IMPORTANT

"I've learned I ain't the smartest guy in the world." (1980)

◆ YOU EARNED IT, BIG GUY

"It's lonely at the top. It's the loneliest place in the world." (1980)

◆ DIDN'T EVEN KNOW NAZARETH HAD A TEAM

"I don't want this happening in the town where I was born."

—after a 14–5 exhibition loss to the Yankees' Columbus Triple A farm team (1978)

◆ THE WILLIAMS COLLEGE ENGLISH DEPARTMENT MUST BE SO PROUD

"I'll tell you this, most of the people who strive and drive aren't particularly loved. But I never tell my people to take the blame while I drink champagne when things are going good. My people know that ultimately I'll take the heat." (1991)

◆ A MAN LOOKS AT HIS LIFE . . . TAKES TWO VALIUM . . . STILL GETS STRESSED

"Look, I'm not saying that I'm a calm, peaceful guy. I'm not Marian the Librarian. I'm a hard-driving guy, and sometimes I get upset." (1991)

◆ A MIND IS A TERRIBLE THING TO WASTE

"I don't know about legend. Maybe 'in his own mind.' "

—about himself, joking with Larry King
(1992)

◆ YOUR HONOR, I'LL ADMIT MY CLIENT HAS HAD A CHECKERED CAREER, HOWEVER . . .

"I've got as many chinks in my armor as anyone."

—on his record (1990)

◆ THE MILK OF HUMAN KINDNESS IS SOAKING OUR CUFFS

"I'd rather be called soft and stupid than a rock and brilliant."

—on rehiring Billy Martin (1978)

◆ IT'S NOT TOO LATE! AND IT'S A GREAT TIME TO BUY!

"I just bought the Cincinnati Reds."

—on Saturday Night Live, minutes after the Reds had won the 1990 World Series

◆ THIS ABOUT SUMS IT UP

"Some guys can lead through real, genuine respect. There are some guys who people would walk through a wall for. OK, but I'm not that kind of a leader. I wish I were." (1987)

◆ IN FACT, I'M SITTING ON NAILS RIGHT HERE AT THIS PRESS CONFERENCE, AND I WON'T SAY IT DOESN'T HURT

"It's tough working for me. I know that. I admit I'm tough on my people. I'm tough on myself." (1992)

◆ I WANT THE WHOLE PIE, AND THE PLATE, AND THE FLATWARE, AND THE TABLE, AND DON'T FORGET I'M LETTING YOU SIT IN MY CHAIR

"I'm not a 49 percent guy."

—on his leadership style (1991)

◆ JUST A WACKY GUY FROM CLEVELAND WITH A DREAM AND A GLARE

"[I'm] your everyday American steely-eyed executive." (1991)

◆ NOT IN ALL CASES

"Nobody likes turmoil or problems, but it makes better people of us."

—after the 1977 season

◆ AND . . . VIOLINS, YOU KICK IN FOR THE BIG FINISH

"There's less time. It's tough. I'm sixty. That's getting up there." (1987)

◆ WHY NOT GET OFF THE INTERSTATE ALTOGETHER?

"I'm going to get to the slow lane—and very shortly." (1987)

◆ NO WONDER. YOU'VE SPENT YOUR LIFE DIGGING YOURSELF OUT OF ONE HOLE AFTER ANOTHER

"The old man's tired."

—on the difficulty of returning to baseball after his Vincent suspension (1991)

◆ IF THIS AIN'T ON TAPE, WE'RE NOT BUYING

"I've always said that if you wait and keep your mouth shut, things will come around right." (1981)

◆ DON'T BE SO HARD ON YOURSELF

"I needed a guy who had worked with young kids. Who could understand their problems and be patient. I don't. I'm too impatient."

—about new Yankee manager Dick Howser (1979)

◆ ANGUISHED BY HIS EFFECT ON OTHERS, THE PRINCIPAL OWNER TAKES A LONG, HARD LOOK INWARD

"Maybe I'm too tough to work for."

—deep in self-analysis, 1989

◆ BUT WITH GOD'S HELP I'LL MAKE IT TO TEN

"On a scale of one to ten, how tense is George Steinbrenner? You can say I rank myself a nine."

—March 1989. It had been, apparently, a difficult winter.

◆ ZEN QUESTION: IS A PARTY A PARTY IF NOBODY SHOWS UP?

"I'm not big on entertaining at home." (1981)

◆ I'VE ALWAYS DEPENDED ON THE KINDNESS OF STRANGERS

"I wish I had class like that, I wish I had the class to go up to a stranger and thank him for something. I don't."

—*on the virtue of humility (1978)*

◆ INTERESTING . . . VERY INTERESTING

"It all comes back to Dad. Whatever good there is in me is him. Whatever bad is me."

◆ YA GET 'EM RIGHT BELOW THE KNEECAPS

"I have a way of bringing guys down to size." (1978)

◆ HYMN THE BOSS

"I make a decision and then I have to go hell-bent for leather. I can't be a nice guy about it. Church choirs are filled with nice guys." (1980)

◆ CIRCLE THE WAGONS, BOYS, THERE'S TROUBLE COMING

"I never dream." (1991)

◆ YEAH, AS A NOSE GUARD

"I'm not your typical owner. I mean, I've worn a jock strap myself." (1991)

◆ YOU COULD, WE WOULDN'T

"I think at times that word could be aptly applied. But just as many times you could apply another word: compassionate."

—*when asked whether he was a bully* (1991)

◆ OVER THE CENTURIES HUMAN BEINGS HAVE STRUGGLED WITH THE NEED TO BE UNDERSTOOD IN THE DEEPEST AND MOST PROFOUND SENSES. THEY HAVE PAINTED, SCULPTED, WRITTEN, AND FOUND MYRIAD WAYS TO EXPRESS THEMSELVES AND AT THE SAME TIME SERVE THEIR FELLOW MAN. MANY HAVE SUCCEEDED. THE BOSS CHOSE TO DESTROY HIS BASEBALL TEAM.

"No one has been able to capture the real me, but I guess it's tough. It's hard for me to convey what I really feel."

—*on misunderstandings* (1987)

◆ BUDDHA'S LISTENING AND HE'S NOT HAPPY

"I'm win-oriented." (1991)

George on Decorum and Tradition

"Why the hell does nobody except me pick up a goddamned thing around here?"

—*upon finding a beer can in the seats at
spring training (1981)*

◆ ETIQUETTE À LA STEINGRABBER

Member of the press: ". . . but isn't some decorum incumbent upon a team owner?"

Steinbrenner: "No, I don't think so." (1991)

◆ NEXT THEY'LL WANT THEIR UNIFORMS CLEANED

"You wouldn't believe the waste I have to put up with."

—*on how many baseballs the Yankees use in a season (1975)*

◆ HAIR TODAY, GONE TOMORROW

"I've got nothing against long hair. But wearing a Yankee uniform represents tradition. After all, I'm paying the bills and issuing the paychecks around here, and I feel a certain way about Yankee tradition."

—*on personal grooming (1989)*

◆ *JAWOHL* HAIR STEINBRENNER

"I want to see the skin above the collar on the backs of their necks."

—on desired hair length for his ballplayers
(1989)

◆ WATCH IT AGAIN, WE THINK YOU MISSED THE MORAL OF THE STORY

"I hate to think how many times I've watched *Pride of the Yankees* on television. I watch it every time it's on." (1981)

◆ AS A CONCEPT, HOWEVER, IT'S BEEN DESPOILED RECENTLY

"The *Pride of the Yankees*, that's it. What a movie."

—Siskel & Ebert commence to worry

◆ AND LOU GEHRIG IS SPINNING IN HIS GRAVE

"My aim when I bought the Yankees was to restore this great team to its former place of prestige. I feel we have done that."

—It should be pointed out that on the day of this quote, July 31, 1990, the Yankees were in last place.

George on Baseball

"I coached football at Northwestern."

◆ DOES HE KNOW THE GAME OR WHAT?

"We needed a left-handed pitcher, and we got one."

> —on the acquisition of right-handed
> pitcher Pat Dobson, May 1973

◆ AND BATS TOO, OR IT'S REALLY HOPELESS

"I'll be a son of a bitch if I'm going to sit up here and sign these paychecks and watch us get our asses kicked by a bunch of rummies. Now, Goddamn it, like they say down on the docks, you got to have balls."

> —after a loss to the Cleveland Indians,
> 1974. The "rummies" on the Indians
> included future Hall of Famers Frank
> Robinson and Gaylord Perry.

◆ I LIKE THE CAJUN ACCENT, THOUGH

"You'll never make it in this league."

> —to pitcher Ron Guidry after a poor
> outing in his second season, 1976. Guidry
> retired with the best winning percentage in
> baseball history—.705.

◆ WELL, SOMETIMES HE'S BRILLIANT, AND SOMETIMES HE'S NOT

"He's a brilliant man on baseball, brilliant."

—on Gabe Paul, Yankee general manager,
April 1977

"I don't mind Gabe leaving with his image intact. But he was in baseball forty years, twenty-five as a GM, and did he ever win a pennant before? You think he made all those moves himself? You think all of a sudden he got brilliant?"

—on Gabe Paul, October 1977

◆ PERHAPS A CASE OF MULTIPLE PERSONALITIES?

"Gabe knows how to get talent. He knows where to get it. He'll fly to Timbuktu in the middle of the night if he thinks he can get a ball player who'll help us."

—Praising Gabe Paul (1978)

"Gabe hasn't got the guts to put a winner on the field. I make all those trades."

—criticizing Gabe Paul (1979)

◆ THE HUMANITARIAN

"I'm afraid some of our players might get hurt playing behind him."

—about pitcher Doyle Alexander after he
lost six straight games (1982)

◆ BUT "NOT PICKED" WAS MY REAL SPECIALTY

"Once in a while, second base; once in a while, out-field."

—answering a question about what position he played in pickup baseball games (1991)

◆ WE KNEW WE SHOULD HAVE READ THE BIBLE MORE RELIGIOUSLY

"I won a championship with my team, and I didn't know anything about baseball. But I bought a good book and I just stayed one page ahead of the team, and that's the way I coached."

—about a high school baseball team he coached (1987)

◆ YOU WORDSMITH, YOU

"I was vociferous in exhorting my coaches and players from the stands. I'd get on their backs when I didn't think they were trying hard enough. I guess over-exuberance, enthusiasm and youth made me the kind of owner that, perhaps, I shouldn't have been."

—about his early days as an owner of the Cleveland Pipers basketball team (1981)

◆ WHO'S ON FIRST . . . WHAT'S IN THE OWNER'S BOX

"The Abbott and Costello of baseball."

> —about Chicago White Sox owners Jerry Reinsdorf and Eddie Einhorn. The jab cost Steinbrenner five grand. (George has also called Reinsdorf and Einhorn "those two pumpkins" and "the Katzenjammer twins.") (1983)

◆ HE MEANT BOB BAILOR MAYBE?

"Baylor's bat will be dead by August."

> —upon trading designated hitter Don Baylor to the Boston Red Sox. That year, 1986, Baylor hit 31 home runs with 94 RBI's. The Red Sox won the pennant.

◆ HOW CAN I EVER THANK YOU?

"I just won you the pennant. I got you Steve Trout."

> —to Yankee manager Lou Piniella in 1986. Trout was 0–4 with a 6.60 era, and the Yanks finished fourth.

◆ WAIT A MINUTE . . . BROOKLYN, I MEANT BROOKLYN!

"I want the Dodgers back in New York, back in the Bronx."

> —after the Yankees had lost the fifth game of the 1981 World Series in Los Angeles. Back in the Bronx, the Dodgers took the sixth game to win the World Series.

◆ AND MAKE SURE YOUR KICKER DOESN'T SPIT THE BIT

"There seems to be an old axiom among baseball people that you have to play for the win on the road. That's a lot of crap! You have to play for the tie first."

—criticizing manager Dick Howser's strategy in not bunting in a late-inning situation (1980)

◆ I EVEN RAN THE PROJECTOR

"I've never seen an athlete so scared. I know athletes. I coached football at Northwestern."

—watching, through binoculars, as reliever Pat Clements warmed up in the bullpen (1987)

◆ SCOUTING LIKE THIS GOT CUSTER KILLED

"Well, maybe he'll do better getting major league hitters out. I don't care. He's coming up and that's it."

—overruling manager Lou Piniella, who opposed bringing struggling minor league pitcher Al Holland up to the Yankees. Holland's 1987 stats after his ascension were disastrous: 6 innings, 9 hits, 9 walks, a 14.61 ERA.

◆ THEIR OWNER WAS SMARTER THAN OUR OWNER

"Their pitcher was better than our pitcher. Their catcher was better than our catcher."

—an in-depth analysis of the 1981 World Series, which the Yankees lost to the Dodgers 4 games to 2

◆ **THEN SOMETIMES THE HITTING'S OKAY, BUT THE PITCHING SUCKS . . . AW, NOTHING'S EVER RIGHT**

"The pitching's okay, but the hitting sucks."

—*after the Yankees split the first two games of a 1985 series against Toronto*

◆ **I WENT INTO SCHWAB'S FOR A FEEN-O-MINT AND . . .**

"I discovered Don Mattingly."

—*The story goes like this: George claims he spotted Mattingly's picture in Sports Illustrated's "Faces in the Crowd" section and recommended to his staff that he be drafted. And it was done. (1987)*

◆ **GOLDEN RETRIEVER OR LABRADOR?**

"Like I told Sparky, how much market value is there for a thirty-four-year-old reliever?"

—*to Cy Young Award winner Sparky Lyle, who forced his trade to the Texas Rangers after the 1978 season by co-writing, with Peter Golenbock, a scathing book, The Bronx Zoo.*

The departure produced one of team wit Graig Nettles's most memorable lines when he said to Lyle:

"You've gone from Cy Young to Sayonara in one year."

◆ AIN'T EXONERATION GRAND?

"I didn't throw those home run balls to Jackson and Grich."

> —George gets tough on pitcher Ron
> Guidry, who allowed three runs in this
> game, memorable for the famous
> "Steinbrenner Sucks" sing-along
> (April 1982)

◆ BUT NOT AS EMBARRASSING AS THE TIME I WAS FINGERPRINTED AND . . . WELL, NEVER MIND

"When Cincinnati swept us in the Series in '76, I vowed to myself that that would never happen again. Now this. I was never so disappointed. It's embarrassing as hell to me. It was even more embarrassing than Cincinnati."

> —after the KC sweep (1980)

◆ AND IF HE DOESN'T WIN . . . HE'S A LOW-DOWN NO-GOOD COMMIE

"He's an all-American boy. Right, Al?"

> —speaking with team president Al Rosen
> about relief pitcher Rawley Eastwick

"He'll be an all-American boy if he wins."

> —Al Rosen, Yankee team president (1978)

◆ BOSS DOES EBERT

"The kind of player I want is the kind who'll have tears in his eyes every time Gary Cooper steps up to that microphone to say, 'I'm the luckiest guy on the face of the earth.' "

> —about the movie of Lou Gehrig's life,
> Pride of the Yankees (1977)

◆ AND IF IT AIN'T, THEN "WE" GUYS IS HISTORY

"I'll make one more change and we think that'll make it right."

> —on tinkering with the team (1983)

◆ THE BUCK STOPS SOMEWHERE ELSE

"We're a true democracy. We sit around a table and I ask each one what he thinks. I don't even vote."

> —on how George makes trade decisions
> with his board of twelve pawn, er, advisers
> (1982)

◆ COME ON, MR. STEINBRENNER, LITTLE TOMMY'S ONLY NINE YEARS OLD

"You're only as good as your last game, If you don't understand that about sports, stay out of the game."

> —deep thoughts about the nature of
> athletics in America (1991)

◆ A FEELING THAT DESERVES ENCOURAGEMENT

"When I don't feel that I want to win for New York Yankee fans, then I'm going to get out of the game."

—a 1991 interview

◆ WHEREAS THREE-QUARTERS BELIEVE YOU'RE FROM MARS

"I don't think so. You go anywhere in the world and people know who the Yankees are. Half the people in the world probably think the Royals are from Canada or something."

—in response to a question asking if he'd consider selling the Yankees

◆ WE SHOULD BE SO LUCKY

"Nah, I'd never sell the Yankees."

—in an interview in 1987

Promises, Promises

"I swear on my heart . . ."

◆ OR ANTI-PERSONNEL MINES FOR DEVELOPING COUNTRIES

"We plan absentee ownership. We're not going to pretend we're something we aren't. I'll stick to building ships."

—at the press conference announcing his syndicate's purchase of the Yankees (1973)

◆ POINT, COUNTERPOINT

"I won't be active in the day-to-day operations of the club."

—upon purchasing the New York Yankees

"I never made any bones about it when I took over the Yankees. I said I'm going to be an involved owner." (1978)

◆ MY FINGERS WERE CROSSED! HA! HA!

"You'll be here as long as I am."

—to Yankee outfielder Bobby Murcer in 1974. Nine months later Murcer was traded to the San Francisco Giants.

◆ THE HORSES DON'T KNOW HOW GOOD THEY GOT IT

"No, I will not be involved in the day-to-day operation of Tampa Bay Downs. With the Yankees and the American Ship Building Company, I just have too much to do. I can't spread myself too thin."

> —upon purchasing a Florida racetrack
> (1980)

◆ THAT GW BRIDGE WILL DO IT TO ANYONE

"I think it's safe to say Dick Howser wants to be a Florida resident the year round."

> —attempting to explain why Howser
> wasn't remaining as Yankee manager.
> Eight months later Howser took another
> managing job—Kansas City. (1980)

◆ IT WAS A TALL, DARK GUY WEARING A TRENCHCOAT—HE'S THE ONE!

"I didn't fire the man."

> —at a press conference announcing Dick
> Howser's resignation as Yankee manager,
> December 1980. Howser's 1980 Yankee
> team won 103 games, the most of any
> Yankee team in the previous twenty years.

◆ FOR SUCCESSFUL LYING, A GOOD MEMORY IS ESSENTIAL

"Firing Dick Howser [and not re-signing Reggie] were the two biggest mistakes I ever made with the Yankees."

—a Steinbrenner statement eulogizing Howser in 1987

◆ FURTHER PROMISES WILL BE FORTHCOMING

"Bob Lemon's going to be our manager all year. You can bet on it. I don't care if we come in last. I swear on my heart he'll be the manager all season."

—on Bob Lemon's managerial status before the 1982 season. Lemon was canned 14 games into the season.

◆ CRUEL AND UNUSUAL PUNISHMENT

"Besides, Bob Lemon is still with me today. He's with me for life." (1991)

◆ BETTER DO IT IN PENCIL

"Dallas Green and Syd Thrift will be there the whole year. You can mark it down."

—quoted in July 1989. Manager Green was fired on August 18. Vice president Thrift resigned under pressure on August 29, 1989.

◆ THAT SWOOSHING SOUND YOU HEAR IS THE AX FALLING

"It's Gabe's decision, he's the smartest man in baseball."

—on the fate of Billy the First

◆ AND THE BEAT GOES ON . . .

"After [1978] Bob Lemon deserves time to show what he can do."

—June 1979. Billy Martin replaced Lemon two weeks later.

◆ AND ON . . .

"I know you've heard this from me before, but Lem's gonna manage for me in '82. There will be no change this year because of the way the team is going. Lem is there and he's staying there."

—December 1981. Lemon, in his second tour, lasted until April 26.

◆ AND ON . . .

"If you want to go out and make a bet, Dallas Green will be sitting in that dugout this year all the way."

—April 1989. Green didn't make it through August.

◆ STILL GOING . . .

"I'm hopeful that Dallas Green knows he's got full control and he'll see that things get done."

◆ AND TOO LATE TO SAVE HIM

"It's too early to get concerned."

—on Dent's future (1990)

◆ TOUGHER THAN AN IRAQI DIPLOMAT ON *NIGHTLINE*

"No, I can't be any more clear about that."

—on manager Bucky Dent's status after five consecutive losses in 1990

◆ THAT OLD SWORD'S ABOUT TO PLUNGE

"You got it!"

—on Syd Thrift's request for independence as general manager (1989)

◆ THAT AND A BUCK TWENTY-FIVE GETS YOU A RIDE ON THE SUBWAY

"I trust that Gene will be around here when they're talking about redoing Yankee Stadium again."

—on Gene Michael, 1980

◆ WHEN WILL I EVER LEARN?

"Great person, great manager. A mistake."

—*on Dick Howser (1991)*

◆ AND AFTER I HIRE HIM AGAIN, I PROBABLY WILL

"I'd do it again."

—*on the firing of Dallas Green (1991)*

◆ AND BUCKY, IN THE BEST MODERN YANKEE TRADITION, KEPT HIS BAGS PACKED

"Bucky Dent will be the manager all year. I'm very strong on loyalties."

—*pledging fidelity to new manager Dent, February 1990. Dent was history by June.*

George on a Certain
Profane Chant

"You think this is funny?"

——————————

On the night of April 27, 1982, Reggie Jackson, whom Steinbrenner had refused to sign, returned to Yankee Stadium for the first time since signing with the California Angels. In his first at-bat that rainy night, against Ron Guidry, he smashed an electrifying home run.

The deliriously happy fans began a spontaneous and thunderous chant directed at the owner's box behind home plate: "Steinbrenner sucks! Steinbrenner sucks!" The chant lasted a full thirty seconds. Some enjoyed the evening. Others did not.

◆ LOUDER!

"I'm sorry, but what did they say? I couldn't quite hear it."

—Ron Guidry to the press after the "Steinbrenner sucks" chant

◆ BUT FUNNY

"I preach mental toughness, so I have to practice it. I thought the word they used was uncouth, though."

—on the "Steinbrenner sucks" chant

◆ THE REST HAD PEOPLE IN THE OLD COUNTRY

"The whole stadium wasn't booing me. Not more than a third to forty-five percent were booing me."

—Gallup-ing

◆ BEFORE SPILLING OUT INTO THE STREETS AND THEN ONTO THE HIGHWAYS OF THIS GREAT LAND, SPREADING, EVER BURGEONING, BRINGING AMERICANS OF ALL RACES, CREEDS AND COLORS TOGETHER IN JOYOUS HARMONY

"It was just a big, unanimous thing that grew until it filled the park."

—on the chant

◆ FOR WHATSOEVER A MAN SOWETH, THAT SHALL HE ALSO REAP (I CORINTHIANS 6:7)

"This is the worst thing that's ever happened to me. . . . How could this happen? . . . How could the fans do this after all I've done for them and this team? I'm humiliated. My family was humiliated . . . I can't believe this . . ."

after the eruption

◆ WE LIKE THE STEINBRENNER SUCKS VERSION BETTER

"You think this is funny? You think this is a god-damned joke? Didn't you hear what they were saying? 'Steinbrenner sucks, Steinbrenner sucks!' You think that's funny? How would you like it if they were chanting 'Torborg sucks, Torborg sucks'?"

—after spotting then Yankee coach (now Met manager) Jeff Torborg unsuccessfully suppressing his laughter

◆ FAN APPRECIATION NIGHT

"It was the only fun I had all night."

—Ron Guidry, after giving up the home run that started the chant that got George mad that got Torborg in trouble and that gave us a chapter in this book

◆ GATOR BAITER

"I didn't expect that from a man I pay $750,000 a year, who gave up a homer to a left-hander who's usually kept out of the line-up against hard-throwing left-handers."

—George on Guidry's comment

The World According to George

"You know, I have a football mentality."

◆ FINE . . . WE'RE SAYING LOSE THE POLYESTER PANTS

"I don't care what people say, you know. They can say what they want."

—*on slings and arrows (1991)*

◆ "THEY" AGAIN

"Winning is everything. I don't care what they tell you." (1992)

◆ TECHNO-WONK GEORGE GETS FRESH

"It's one more advantage for your side, and that's what sports are all about."

—*on equipping Yankee personnel with walkie-talkies*

◆ FREUD, MOVE ATTA THE WAY

"He's scared stiff. Gutless."

—*on rookie Jim Beattie during a June 1976 game with the Red Sox. Beattie was sent to the minors—during the game.*

◆ I GOT A FEELING THIS COULD BE THE START OF A BEAUTIFUL FRIENDSHIP

"Why don't you bring your boy down to spring training with the Yankees?"

> —1972. To James Polk, a reporter beginning an investigation into what would prove to be Steinbrenner's illegal campaign contribution to Richard Nixon.

◆ THE DISCREET ART OF FRIENDLY PERSUASION

"You better not play that tape on the air. Let me tell you, I'm on the [major league baseball] television committee and NBC will get shit all over."

> —to Mike Weisman, an NBC sports producer, regarding a controversial taped interview scheduled for the Game of the Week that Steinbrenner was trying to kill

◆ AND IF YOU'RE ON THE COUCH FIVE TIMES A WEEK, YOU COULD REALLY MAKE SOME PROGRESS . . . HELL, PRETTY SOON YOU'RE OUT OF THE HOSPITAL ALTOGETHER AND BACK IN BASEBALL WHERE YOU WANNA BE!

"You get talking and you don't recall why you're doing it. You tell him what you're thinking."

> —about a conversation with Howie Spira that we thought for a second was from a session with a shrink . . . but we were mistaken and anyway everybody knows that's privileged information and we don't want to break any laws or confidences or do anything wrong at all . . . but didn't Howie Spira major in . . . aw, never mind (1990)

◆ AND THE "CONTRARIAN SOCIETY" PRESENTS ITS CONTRARIAN-OF-THE-CENTURY AWARD TO . . .

"Anybody who's around me probably has differences with me. That's me."

> *—after hiring Gene Michael as Yankee manager in the winter of 1980.*

◆ VALENTINO SPEAKS

"Winning 103 games is like kissing your sister. It's nice, but it doesn't pack the wallop that kissing your girlfriend does."

> *—after the Yanks lost the 1980 American League Championship to Kansas City in a three-game sweep*

◆ YEOW . . . I ARE AUTHOR

"It has been my thought and desire for a long time that someday I would write a book, not just about baseball but about everything I have been involved with. . . . I think I would write a book that would be so enlightening in so many areas that it could be a great seller."

> *—in a letter to writer Dick Schaap (1981)*

◆ FOR EXAMPLE, FIRING THEM FROM THEIR PAPER ROUTES WILL TEACH AN IMPORTANT LESSON ABOUT LIFE'S VICISSITUDES

"What I have been through in my lifetime I would like to think that many needy people, particularly the young kids who it is my plan to benefit, would benefit."

—*further along in the letter to Schapp*

◆ PERCEPTION-IS-REALITY DEPARTMENT

"Frank Cashen wouldn't have the guts to say whether he really said it, but I believe he did."

—*After the Met general manager made a supposedly off-the-record joke about comparing the movie Fort Apache to Yankee Stadium (1980)*

◆ AND WHAT WE NEED ARE VENUS FLYTRAPS

"He's a morning glory. That's a term we use for a horse who is great in the morning workouts, who looks beautiful, but who can't do it in the race. The horse spits the bit, and Ken Clay has spit the bit."

—*About a rookie pitcher (1977)*

◆ JUST IN CASE IT SLIPPED ANYBODY'S MIND

"And keep in mind, I'm the guy who signs your paychecks."

—*after asking his Yankee team to vote for drug testing (1985)*

◆ FEEDING ADMIRALS TO SHARKS IS ALWAYS A GAS

"But keep in mind—keep in mind—there's only one admiral on this ship. There may be some vice-admirals, but only one admiral. So let's get out there and have some fun!!!"

> —to his Yankee team after a compromise
> on the Yankees' attitude toward drug
> testing (1985)

WORLDS APART

Selections from a colloquy between pitcher Goose Gossage and a blindly optimistic boss.

PRINCIPAL OWNER: "I'm very hopeful of signing Goose again. I think Goose belongs in New York."

GOOSE GOSSAGE: "I have no interest in any contract offer from George Steinbrenner."

PRINCIPAL OWNER: "I think Goose is a cinch for the Hall of Fame if he stays in New York."

GOOSE GOSSAGE: "I will not return to play for George Steinbrenner."

> —December 1983. Gossage, a
> passionate, volatile man, was a life-long
> Yankee fan who had always dreamed of
> playing in New York. With his departure
> and that of Graig Nettles, both to the
> Padres, and the retirement of Lou Piniella,
> the season of 1983 marked the
> end of an era.

◆ FIND THE ONES THAT DO AND WE'RE TALKING PULITZER

"My horses don't talk to the press." (1985)

◆ AWE-FUL

"They had these gray uniforms, but there was a blue hue to them. I'll never forget them. Watching them warm up was as exciting as watching the game. Being in Cleveland, you couldn't root for them, but you could boo them in awe."

—Steinbrenner on his Cleveland youth in awe of the Yankees (1977)

◆ RUSH LIMBAUGH BREATHES A SIGH OF RELIEF

"They call me a flaming liberal, I guess that's what I am." (1981)

◆ OH, SO THAT'S WHO HE IS

"I'll meet with the mayor, he's the leader of the city."

—on how he proposed to handle New York City's complaint that the Yankees pay far too little in rent ($150,000 per annum) for Yankee Stadium (1981)

◆ MILLARD FILMORE, CALVIN COOLIDGE, GERALD FORD. THESE GUYS DONE GOOD, TOO

"Believe me, I'm no isolationist, but I admire Taft."

—The Boss discoursing on American foreign policy (1981)

◆ KILL 'EM ALL. AND LET GOD SORT 'EM OUT

"In these countries that shoot at our embassies, if I was president, I would say I'm cutting your ass off right now. From now on you get nothing. Not even a smile."

—on diplomatic philosophy (1981)

◆ BEWARE THE TEARS OF CROCODILES

"If you watch these young men and women on the awards stand when the National Anthem of this country is played, if you don't cry, you're not an American."

—after the Summer Olympics in Barcelona (1992)

◆ JUST A GUESS, BUT PERHAPS BONNIE BLAIR WAS TRYING TO AVOID BOORISH TYCOONS WHO CALL HER "GIRL"

"It's imperative that we do right by our athletes. When I see what that girl from Champaign, Illinois, has done and then read that she used to have to sneak into the rink at 6:00 A.M. to practice, there's something wrong."

—after George was appointed to chair a commission to review the effectiveness of the U.S. Olympic committee (1988)

◆ GEORGE DOES GRUNGEWEAR

"I don't believe in taking my government to the cleaners."

—on suspected cost overruns in government bidding on shipbuilding projects (1990)

◆ THAT SOUND YOU JUST HEARD WAS SWEDEN EXHALING

"I'm not interested in socialism." (1983)

◆ AND AS LONG AS YOU DRY 'EM OUT THOROUGHLY, THEY BURN CLEAN

"Kids are our greatest natural resource—greater than oil, greater than gas, greater than coal." (1991)

◆ THEN COMES FIRING MINIONS, FOLLOWED BY HOT DOGS AND GOING POTTY

"Winning is the second greatest thing in the world next to breathing." (1990)

◆ WOW, TALK ABOUT GOOFY

"There's nothing more American than Mickey Mouse, Billy Martin, George Steinbrenner, and Goofy." (1985)

◆ THOSE WHO FORGET THE PAST ARE CONDEMNED TO REPEAT IT DEPARTMENT

"It's just the book I happened to pick up, I love to learn about battles and victors."

> —on reading a book about Custer's last stand when Fay Vincent was deciding whether or not to ban him from baseball.

◆ WE TALKING PATTON?

"I don't know anyone who is perfect since that guy who walked on water."

> —defending a college football coach who'd been fired (1987)

◆ THE FIRST PERSON WHO TELLS YOU NOT TO USE A CHUTE . . . HE'S THE TRAITOR!

"I think I'm dangerous enough right now. But some people have said I should take up skydiving. I'm very suspect of them." (1991)

◆ GEORGE STEINBRENNER. ABRAHAM LINCOLN. CUT FROM THE SAME CLOTH. NOT!

"You think Lincoln was popular? Lincoln said, 'I do the very best I can. If the end brings me out right, what is said against me won't amount to anything. If the end brings me out wrong, ten angels swearing I was right would make no difference.' I have that sign up in my office, at Yankee Stadium, in my bedroom, everywhere." (1990)

◆ NOW LET US GET THIS STRAIGHT . . . HEAD FIRST, THEN FEATHERS?

"That chicken would run around with no head. Suddenly he'd flop down and you had to pick the feathers."

—on chopping off chicken heads when he was nine years old in the poultry business his father gave him instead of an allowance (1992)

◆ WHICH IS WHY WE LOCK UP SHARP OBJECTS

"The only thing that can hurt us is ourselves."

—on good PR (1977)

◆ BUT MAYBE YOU CAN BUY IT

"I mean you can't create the perfect racehorse."

—philosophizing on the potential for human perfection (1991)

◆ SOMETIMES "THEY" REALLY ARE OUT TO GET YOU

"My horse was running well, but at one point on the track they used some darker dirt or something. When my horse and another horse got there, they jumped the darker dirt and lost stride."

—on why his horse, Steve's Friend, (29 to 1 shot) lost the 1977 Derby to Seattle Slew

◆ OTHER THAN THAT PHONE CALL FROM FAY . . . OR BOWIE . . . OR THE FEDERAL PROSECUTOR'S OFFICE

"It's the scariest feeling I've ever had."

—on driving a harness cart (1992)

◆ WOW! COOL . . .

"Different strokes for different folks. Different rhythms for different times."

—on the New George (1990)

◆ A MIND LIKE A STEEL TRAP

"I remember one time I went to school accidentally carrying two eggs in my jacket and they squashed in my pockets. I can remember little things like that."

—on memories of childhood (1981)

◆ WHY JUST THE GLIDER?

"I'll bet you could get every guy on the team to put up $1,000 each just to get me up there, and then one of them would stand there with the rifle and—bang—shoot the glider."

—free-associating while watching a hang glider in Florida (1978)

◆ OR IF WE WERE IN A LESS PUBLIC PLACE—SAY, AN ELEVATOR

"If you were a little bigger, I'd punch you out."

—to veteran horseman Eddie McKinsey. McKinsey reported that he answered, "You don't have the heart to punch me out." No fight ensued. (1980)

◆ BUT THAT SUMBITCH WHO STOLE MY FLEA COLLAR IS MEAT

"I don't mind being the underdog." (1989)

◆ MAY WE SUGGEST DESKTOP BUNGEE JUMPING . . .

"You don't do enough dangerous things."

—discussing the perils of the sedentary lives many businessmen live (1987)

◆ MAY WE SUGGEST BATTING PRACTICE BLINDFOLDED?

"I'm not saying everybody should go out and do something dangerous. But you should do something a little dangerous every once in a while. A little something exciting. A little something of a personal, physical challenge." (1987)

◆ BIGGER, SMALLER, DON'T MATTER . . . LONG AS I GOT MY GUYS

"One always thinks that he can handle any situation that may occur. And I'm certainly not intimidated by any guy whether he's bigger than I or smaller than I. That's not been my history." (1987)

◆ YA SPITS ON DA YANKS, YA SPITS ON ME

"I clocked them. There are two guys in this town looking for their teeth."

—on his alleged fight with two Dodger fans in an elevator during the 1981 World Series. Reggie Jackson offered the opinion that the opponents were probably in their preteens.

◆ CHECK OUT THESE CALVINS, MARKY MARK!

"I'd stand up, go behind the chair, drop my drawers, he'd stick a needle in, and boom! I mean, what the f**k am I going to say? 'Oh, fellows, you have to get out, he's going to give me a shot.' F**k that! Call it macho, call it what you like, I don't give a shit."

—describing a B-12 shot he would sometimes receive during meetings (1991

◆ BUT JUST IN CASE, KEEP THESE BRASS KNUCKLES IN YOUR LUNCH BOX

"Don't get in any fights if you don't have to. I wouldn't like it."

—sage advice to a nine-year-old

◆ LOVE AND RESPECT ARE OVERRATED ANYWAY

"I hope I don't lead through fear, and I would hope it was more love and respect, but maybe it isn't."

—on his business style (1981)

◆ TAKE FATTY ARBUCKLE, FOR EXAMPLE

"There has to be a heavy in everything. This country didn't get where it is without a lot of heavies." (1990)

◆ ANTARCTICA'S GOT MAJOR PROBLEMS . . . HOW 'BOUT STARTING THERE?

"I'm going to get active in a lot of places because I don't find what's happening acceptable. No way."

—on Yankees poor performance (1990)

◆ MAKE IT THE CHUMP AND WE'RE WITH YOU

"The buck stops with me. I am the chief."

—taking the blame for letting Reggie Jackson leave the Yankees after the 1981 season

◆ HE'S THE PORTLY FELLOW WITH THE ICE CREAM CONE WHO DOESN'T LIKE YOU

"[Henderson will find out] who the boss is."

—warning for Ricky Henderson when he was about to rejoin the Yankees after an injury (1985)

◆ **EVEN IF THAT MEANS SUSPENSIONS, BIG FINES, RIDICULE, SCORN, CONDEMNATION**

"You just have to do it in your way."

—*On leadership (1987)*

◆ **A WHOLE NEW CASTE OF CHARACTERS?**

"I finished fifth. Teams that finish there don't have untouchables."

—*after the 1988 season*

◆ **SELF-AWARENESS IS THE KEY TO SUCCESS**

"I'm more of a Patton than an Eisenhower in the way I lead. Maybe that's a fault. I don't know. But that's the way I am. I can't change it and be effective." (1990)

◆ **UND IF VE DO, I VILL NOT SHADDUP MEIN TRAPP UNT TIL I AM BLUE IN ZE FACE-IN. AT VICH POINT VE VILL COMMENCE SPRINK TRAININK EIN FEBRVARY EIN GREENLAND.**

"We will not allow our team to get blown out of this race." (1987)

◆ I'D LIKE TO THANK THE LITTLE PEOPLE EVERYWHERE

"Maybe the silk-stocking guys don't like the way I run this ball club, but the little guy—the bartender, the guy pushing a car, the cabdrivers—they're the ones who need the Yankees." (1977)

◆ WE DIDN'T KNOW YOU CARED

"The poor soul, I bet he hasn't seen ten baseball games in ten years."

> —on Barrister Simons, then the director of
> the Office of Collective Bargaining for the
> city of New York, who arbitrated the
> Cerone dispute in 1981

◆ NOBLESSE OBLIGE

"Class, what class they have."

> —on the average man (1978)

◆ AND THEY BOOED FROM THE ROOFTOPS

"I've been to the South Bronx."

> —on travel (1978)

◆ GET NAKED OR KILL SOMEBODY? AREN'T THERE OTHER OPTIONS? WHAT ABOUT TEAM LOYALTY? WHAT ABOUT LOVE OF THE GAME?

"You have to understand the mentality of the sports fan. When soccer fans riot and kill people over the score of a game, when baseball fans jump down from the stands, run onto the field and strip, that's just their nature." (1991)

◆ DON'T WORRY, YOU DON'T

"Now look, I'm no crusader, I don't want to sound like that." (1991)

◆ SOLID, BRO

"I'm no Robin Hood. I just like to help people. That's my bag."

—on his inclination for altruism (1991)

◆ WHAT IS THERE TO SAY?

"You show me a good loser and I'll show you a loser." (1990)

◆ COUNT YOUR BLESSINGS. IN JAPAN, YOU'D THEN RESIGN AND BE THINKING ABOUT HARI-KARI. THANK GOD FOR AMERICA!

"I'm embarrassed. I apologize to the city of New York."

—after a 2–4 1977 road trip. The Yankees won the World Series later that year.

◆ FIRE YOUR SIMILE WRITER . . . THEN LIE DOWN AND CHILL

"I felt sorry for Bucky. He looked like General Custer riding into the ambush at Little Big Horn."

—after the Mets, using their regulars, defeated the Yankees 11–0 in a spring training game (1990)

◆ GLUTTONS FOR PUNISHMENT

"They weren't even worth watching!"

—on Yankees' poor play against the White Sox, August 3, 1982. Steinbrenner said all 34,000 fans in the stadium could come to another game free.

◆ STIFLE YOURSELF

"I'm like Archie Bunker, I get mad as hell when my team blows one."

—Archie, a class act, was a Mets fan (1981)

◆ TRUST YOUR GUT

"I really don't know. I'd have to take some time to think."

—*when asked if he was bad for baseball
(1985)*

◆ AND THREE YEARS LATER WHEN I GAVE HIM THE TWO-YEAR, $1.8 MILLION CONTRACT . . .

"Definitely fat and probably finished."

—*about Graig Nettles, who said in
response:*

"That irritated me, but I have to consider the source. It comes from a man who obviously knows nothing about how to control his weight. Two things he knows nothing about are baseball and weight control." (1980)

◆ GOD, IT WAS LIKE THE MOST WONDERFUL, LOVELY DREAM. . . . THEN THE DUGOUT PHONE WOKE ME UP

"I told my people, 'Stick doesn't want your interference, so we won't interfere with him. Don't call him anymore. Don't interfere with him. Stay away from him.' "

—*explaining why he ordered Yankee
employees to give manager Gene
Michael the silent treatment during the
1981 season*

◆ WHEN LIFE GIVES YOU LEMONS, MAKE LEMONADE

"We had a strategy. Lemon chose to ignore it."

> —criticizing his manager's tactics in the
> 1981 World Series. The opponents, the
> Dodgers, out-hit and out-pitched the
> Yankees.

◆ COULD BE THE M.S.G.

"No way they [the Chinese] could have improved so dramatically in just four years [without steroids]."

> —about the Chinese Olympic women's
> swimming team (1992)

◆ DID I SAY THAT? I COULDN'T HAVE SAID THAT. AND IF I DID SAY IT, I DIDN'T MEAN IT. I LIKE FLORIDA.

"Nothing but a bunch of old folks over there and a rickety bridge to get there."

> —reported by St. Petersburg City council
> member Bill Bond, Jr., as a Steinbrenner
> comment on the city as a possible site for
> a major league franchise. Critics accused
> Steinbrenner of trying to "wreck" the city's
> chances of getting a team. Steinbrenner
> later denied the above quote.

◆ DEFINITELY A LONG SHOT, BUT WE THINK HE'D LOOK GREAT IN A BLANKET AND FEEDBAG

"I could have run faster than my horse down the stretch."

—joking about a celebrity harness race in which he drove (1991)

◆ WE BELIEVE A GAG ORDER FOR THE PRINCIPAL OWNER WOULD SAIL THROUGH THE SUPREME COURT

"But why shouldn't I speak out? Don't you speak out in this country?" (1991)

◆ ASK ANYBODY WHO'S WORKED FOR ME

"Things aren't often as they appear."

—appearing on Nightline (1990)

◆ PEOPLE IN GLASS HOUSES . . .

"I just can't understand all these teams changing managers the way they do. The lack of stability is alarming." (1985)

◆ MAMA MacPHAIL DIDN'T RAISE NO FOOL

"He doesn't know how to open the box, damn it."

—on why American League president Lee MacPhail wouldn't take his telephone call (which was about a bad umpiring decision during a game at Yankee Stadium). George sent a boy to MacPhail's seat to show him how to open the telephone box. (1978)

◆ AND THIS MAN KNOWS BULL WHEN HE HEARS IT

"When they point at the Yankees, it's pure bull. You look at the top ten salaries in baseball, and not one of them are the Yankees."

—commenting on big-spending fellow owners (1990)

◆ BET THE RANCH!

"Maybe he knows something I don't."

—after Don Mattingly was quoted saying he felt the Yankees would probably deal him because of recent comments (1988)

◆ POP THE CORKS, BREAK OUT THE BELUGA, WE GOT A REASON TO CELEBRATE

"I'm backing off, I've got to back off. I mean it this time. I'm clamming up. I'm off, as of now. If they want me to shut up, fine, I'll shut up."

—after ripping his three best players, Dave Winfield, Don Mattingly and Rickey Henderson, on the day of the All-Star game, no less. (He later apologized that "it came out wrong about Mattingly.") (1988)

◆ BITCH, BITCH, BITCH . . . NOTHING'S EVER RIGHT

"The president, in his infinite wisdom, didn't choose enough outfielders. Two of the reserves he picks are Larry Parrish and Pat Tabler. They say those guys can't play the outfield. That's ridiculous; I've seen them play the outfield."

—complaining, after Winfield played 13 innings in the All-Star game, about American League President Bobby Brown (1987)

◆ STRESSED TO KILL

"Now the pressure is on him to lead us to the World Series. He's no longer just a little Hoosier from Indiana."

—after Don Mattingly was awarded $1.97 million in salary arbitration (1987)

◆ BUT I'VE PURCHASED A NEW MOOD RING AND FIRMLY BELIEVE THINGS WILL BE DIFFERENT

"I can't make excuses for the turnover, we've had a lot." (1989)

◆ RUN YOUR MOUTH. WRITE A CHECK

"I wouldn't want to be Lee MacPhail living in New York. Maybe he should go house hunting in Kansas City."

> —an outburst about the American League president after he ruled against the Yankees in the "pine tar" game. The comment cost The Boss a cool, fifty large. (1983)

◆ TWO? NAME 'EM

"When you're down, you don't want to see your friends, you don't want to go to places and restaurants. Human nature is funny. When you're down, a lot of people walk the other way. You find out who your two friends are."

> —philosophizing after his Cleveland Piper basketball team went into bankruptcy (1962)

◆ HE EVEN FIRES OTHER PEOPLE'S EMPLOYEES

"Whoever made the decision to put in extra field seats down the left-field foul line at Shea for the playoffs probably won't do it again—that is, if he's still around."

> —writing about the 1986 World Series, in which temporary stands prevented Mets' shortstop Rafael Santana from catching a foul pop. Houston's Alan Ashby got a second life and hit a home run. (1986)

◆ METS ENVY

"I'm impressed with the Mets organization. They certainly have a great organization. We're reorganizing everything. We have new people in scouting, in the front office. We're revamping everything. Now we'll see what happens. I think we'll pick up. It might take a while."

—1989. So far progress has been slow.

◆ CHECK HIS BUBBA LICENSE

"Here we have a fellow who doesn't come with a heck of a lot of glamour. For the first five years I knew him, I kept calling him 'Lump.' He was madder than hell."

—on his new manager Stump Merrill
(1990)

◆ THIS IS A WITTY LINE AND WE'RE GIVING CREDIT WHERE CREDIT IS DUE. ATTA BOY, GEORGE!

"If I wanted my players to learn Ping-Pong, I'd send them to China."

—after the Yankees played a game on
artificial turf (1987)

◆ SIGH ... MORE GIVE CREDIT WHERE IT'S DUE DEPARTMENT (DON'T WORRY—IT'S A SHORT CHAPTER!)

" 'He ruined my life!' Could have fooled me. I thought it was one of those do-it-yourself kits."

—quoting Howard Spira, then commenting. In testimony against the con man. (1991)

◆ DANNY, A MET OUTFIELDER, HAD NINE CAREER RBI'S IN THE MAJORS ... DIDN'T EVEN KNOW HE PLAYED AT WATERLOO

"I'm not going to mention anyone by name, but there are some guys on my team who have left more guys stranded than Napoleon at Waterloo." (1985)

◆ PROOF POSITIVE THAT JOCKS DON'T READ

"I guess they'd never been around a man who was thrown out of baseball."

—on his popularity with American athletes at the Olympic games, who all wanted photos taken with The Boss (1991)

◆ CAN THIS MAN TELL A JOKE OR WHAT?

"My good friend Bo called me and asked me if I believed in free speech. I said I certainly did. He said, 'Fine, you're giving one at the Naval Academy.' "

—relating a conversation with J. O. "Bo" Coppedge, athletic director at the United States Naval Academy (1991)

◆ AND SOME WHO DIDN'T

"We beat everybody who showed up."

> —when asked, after the 1978 Series, how
> the Yankees could claim to be world
> champions when only teams from the
> United States and Canada were
> represented

◆ QUACK, QUACK, HE SHOT ME DOWN

"The Goose should do more pitching and less quacking."

> —about pitcher Rich Gossage (1978)

◆ YOU GO ON AHEAD. JUST LEAVE THE REVOLVER AND THE EXTRA CANTEEN

"Don't worry about me. I'm fine. Just keep playing good baseball. You're doing great right now. Keep it up. I'm behind you one hundred percent, and my thoughts are with you and will continue to be with you every day."

> —on the day of his resignation, in a phone
> call quoted by then Yankee manager
> Stump Merrill (1990)

George's Malapropisms

*"Baseball is ninety percent mental.
The other half is physical."*

—*Yogi Berra*

◆ THAT ENIGMATIC SIMILE

"Owning the Yankees is like owning the *Mona Lisa*. That's something you never see."

—on whether he would ever sell the team (1981)

◆ ALTHOUGH BADLY BUTCHERED, JOHN DRYDEN WILL SURVIVE . . . AND DEMAND TO BE TRADED

"You are wounded but you are not slain. You will lay down and bleed awhile. But by God, I'll bet you will rise and fight again."

—misquoted, with feeling, from Dryden's "Johnnie Armstrong's Last Goodnight," which is inscribed on a gift given to George after the Yankees finished fourth in the 1979 season

◆ WE BELIEVE THE QUOTE IS "LIKE A *WOMAN* SCORNED" . . . BUT WE'RE NOT STICKLERS

"I feel like a father scorned. I feel like I have a son who has done something wrong and isn't mature enough to admit it."

> —reacting to Gene Michael, who had popped off at Steinbrenner during the 1981 season. Michael was fired the next day.

◆ THE YANKEE CLIPPER

"A schooner doesn't make many knots in a calm sea. Of course, I'm not looking for a tornado like last year."

> —commenting on the tumultuous 1977 season during the spring of 1978

◆ BUT GOSH, THE GUY'D HAVE A GREAT AVERAGE . . .

"If a guy got a hit every time he went to the plate, there would be no fun in baseball." (1987)

George on Crime and Punishment

"We're not worried about it."

◆ A COUPLE FIBS, YEAH, BUT POSITIVELY NO LIES

"I never asked them to lie."

> —commenting to reporters on his legal
> problems with campaign contributions,
> January 1973. On November 27, 1974,
> Bowie Kuhn, then the commissioner of
> Baseball, said in suspending Steinbrenner
> from baseball: "Attempting to influence
> employees to behave dishonestly is the
> kind of misconduct which, if ignored by
> baseball, would undermine the public's
> confidence in our game."

◆ AND MY BUDDY SPIRO, HE AIN'T GUILTY OF NUTHIN' NEITHER

"No one wants to go through the agony of a trial, but
I feel strongly I must stand and fight for what I believe
is right. I am confident that I will be found innocent
of the charges."

> —commenting on a pending court case,
> April 5, 1974. Four months later, August
> 23, 1974, Steinbrenner pleaded guilty to
> two felony counts: conspiracy to violate
> the campaign contributions law and
> aiding and abetting obstruction of an
> investigation.

◆ **HONEST TO GOD, AND THIS IS JUST BETWEEN YOU AND ME, I SWEAR I DIDN'T KNOW IT WAS WRONG!!**

"[It was a] fifty-seven-year-old law that nobody really knew much about in those days."

—explaining how his inept lawyers gave him bad advice which led to his 1974 felony conviction

◆ **THOUGH YOU BETTER WATCH OUT FOR SOME OF THOSE PESKY LAWS WHICH CAN RESULT IN ANNOYING FELONY CONVICTIONS**

"Be the uncommon man and woman. Don't worry too much about what you think society dictates, because it's the uncommon men of this country that have led it to greatness."

—to the graduating class of the Massachusetts Maritime Academy 1981

◆ **IN THE OLD DAYS YOU WOULDA SEEN MY WHOLE FIST IN THE PIE, NOW IT'S JUST A FINGER**

"I was much too involved, too strong. This year I've held back."

—May 1983. Just for the record, during the season Steinbrenner was fined $50,000 and suspended a week for criticizing the umpires. His manager, Billy Martin, was suspended twice. It was the first time in baseball history a manager and owner were suspended in the same season.

◆ **AND I PROMISE NEVER, EVER TO MAKE ILLEGAL CONTRIBUTIONS TO RICHARD NIXON'S RE-ELECTION CAMPAIGN AGAIN, AND I WON'T COVER IT UP IF I GET CAUGHT, EITHER.**

"I'm very grateful."

—after being pardoned by Ronald Reagan, in the latter's last week in office

◆ **AND CLINTON HAS NO SHOT. ZERO.**

"None whatsoever, according to my people. We're not worried about it."

—about the possibility of suspension in the Howie Spira incident (1990)

◆ **HANG IN THERE, IT'LL ALL BECOME CLEAR**

"I'm having trouble agreeing with the whole investigation as things come out day after day."

—commenting on the Howie Spira investigation (1990)

◆ **DIDN'T WE HEAR SOMETHING LIKE THIS ON THE WHITE HOUSE TAPES?**

"I thought I did it the legal and proper way. I said, 'I want this thing done legally, nothing's going to be hidden.' I said, 'You take care of it.' "

—on the $40,000 check to Howie Spira (1990)

◆ SAY WHAT?

"I'm happy with it. I'm satisfied with the resolution of it."

—commenting on Fay Vincent
"permanently" banning him from baseball
(1990)

◆ KILL THE UMPIRE!
DON'T, THEY CRIED, YOU'LL BE SUSPENDED!

"I don't think anyone should be suspended for life for anything other than murder." (1990)

George on the Media

"Don't believe it, they lied."

———————————————

◆ **AH, WE REMEMBER THE HEADLINES WELL: "BRONX ZOO TO ADD 'ANGRY FAT GUY FROM CLEVELAND' EXHIBIT"**

"To compete for the entertainment dollar, particularly in New York, you have to have more than nine guys playing baseball; you've got to have an attraction. And I have tried to do the best job I possibly can to give my fans an 'attraction.'" (1983)

◆ **GEORGE FROM CLEVELAND WHO LIVES IN TAMPA IS ON THE LINE**

"To make it in New York you have to suffer the slings and arrows of outrageous fortune." (1992)

◆ **WITH POWER TOOLS, AUTOMATIC WEAPONS, TRUNCHEONS, AND BROKEN UMBRELLAS**

"The press has created that perception. Walk down the street with me sometime in New York. Construction workers, cops, cabbies, doormen, they all come up and tell me they're behind me."

—*on his tumbling image (1990)*

◆ BUT THEY'RE A BITCH TO GET IN THE LOCK

"Television is the key to all sports." (1991)

◆ MAYBE, LIKE, SPREADING OUT MORE BANANA PEELS?

"Hey, can I help you guys?"

> —to photographers who fell chasing him
> as he stormed off after his banning (1989)

◆ SOUNDS LIKE TONY DREW BLOOD

"How's this for the mouth that bites the hand that feeds it?"

> —complaining about broadcaster and
> former star Yankee shortstop Tony Kubek,
> who had criticized him for making players
> "fear for their jobs" (1978)

◆ HE'S SEMI-TOUGH, HE CAN HANDLE IT . . .

"How can you sit with that little shit?"

> —to writer Dan Jenkins, who was having
> dinner at Elaine's, a bistro on New York's
> upper East Side, with columnist Mike
> Lupica (1980)

◆ WISHFUL THINKING, DUDE

"Mike is talented, and he's a good writer, but I think he made a bad mistake (leaving the *New York Daily News* to go to *The National*). He's not read anywhere. Nobody knows him anymore. People have forgotten Mike Lupica and, in that business, you fade in a hurry."

> —Lupica, one of Steinbrenner's harsher critics, has returned to the Daily News; he also writes a column for Esquire, is a regular on ESPN's The Sports Reporters, and a bestselling mystery novelist. Otherwise, no one knows him anymore. (1991)

◆ EVERYWHERE I LOOK, THERE'S A SUBPOENA!

"Like you guys have been telling me, it's a trial down there."

> —to reporters in the locker room during spring training, discussing how difficult it is to keep his mouth shut (1978)

◆ HMMM . . . WE *WOULD* LIKE TO SELL LOTS OF BOOKS

"Yeah, see? F**k that stuff. Don't believe it; they lied. Sportswriters have to create sensationalism to sell their damn books. You can't sell a book unless you stretch a point. If it doesn't make Steinbrenner out to be a big ogre—if it makes him a nice guy—they don't want that, because it doesn't sell."

> —responding to question about reporters portraying him as unstable (1991)

◆ WHY WE SHOULD APPRECIATE OUR PUSHY, NOSY NEW YORK MEDIA

"If I thought I could get away with it in New York, I'd do it."

—*about trading Don Mattingly (1990)*

◆ WE'RE NOT TOUCHING THIS WITH A TEN-FOOT POLE

"'We want to portray you as Adolph Hitler.' I said no to that."

—*answering a suggestion from Saturday Night Live writers (1990)*

◆ NOT COUNTING THAT FEDERAL INDICTMENT . . .

"I have never read such irresponsible crap."

—*about stories saying Don Mattingly's back injury was career-threatening (1989)*

◆ STAY OUT OF THE BARNYARD

"I'm tired of the bullshit." (1991)

◆ EXCUSE US?

"I won't comment on that, because there were times when I probably did."

—*on being accused of leaking information as a "top Yankee official" (1991)*

◆ AND WE NOW ANNOUNCE THE PERMANENT RETIREMENT OF THE "POT CALLING THE KETTLE BLACK" TROPHY

"I'm damn tired of the crap that gets printed that have as their only basis 'sources said' or 'said one agent' without a name next to that quote."

> —*reacting to article in the New York Post predicting that free agents would avoid New York because of a "fear factor"* (1988)

◆ ALWAYS WORKS WONDERS WITH THE EMPLOYEES

"Guys in the smaller TV markets are saying the Yankees are in the big market. I'm being a good boy. We didn't break the $3-million (a-year) barrier; Gene Autry did in California. And then Oakland. Then who breaks the record is Kansas City. The next time [Royal owner] Ewing Kauffman says they don't have the market to compete with me, I'll say, 'Sit down and shut up.' " (1990)

◆ WE LIKE TO RESERVE THAT FOR YANKEE STADIUM

"I didn't want to put down New York."

> —*rejecting a Saturday Night Live sketch* (1990)

George on Ice Cream

"Taste the vanilla."

◆ AND ALL THE FOLKS AT BEN AND JERRY THANK YOU FOR IT

"I'll tell you the truth. I go to the icebox, I take out a whole pint of ice cream, and eat it all. And that's why I'm as heavy as I am."

—talking about his response to the frustration of not being able to participate in running the Yankees (1992)

◆ ALL THE FOLKS IN ORGANIZED RELIGION THANK YOU

"Ice cream is my salvation."

—how he deals with Yankee miscues (1992)

◆ FAT, DUMB, AND HAPPY

"You've got to taste the vanilla. It's really good. It's smooth, not too grainy. It used to be grainy, but I told them I wanted it just like the ice cream at the jai-alai. Really smooth. And they've got it now. Taste it. See, smooth." (1981)

◆ **SWEET REVENGE**

"You're never going to see Chipwiches again on our plane."

—*after a disagreement with Astro owner John McMullen, a major ice cream sandwich stockholder (1974)*

"HOTEL OWNER GOES BERSERK"
"FAULTY FREEZER BLAMED"
"CHEF TRADED"

"There was no excuse for those ice chunks in the ice cream. I demanded to know who was in charge of the food quality."

—*on dessert quality at the Bay Harbor Inn, which he owns (1981)*

◆ **HEY, I GOT HUMAN FEELINGS JUST LIKE EVERYBODY ELSE**

"I'm hurt about Goose calling me the 'Fat Man.' I'm really trying to lose weight."

—*after being blasted by Yankee relief pitcher Goose Gossage who, among other things, said:*

"I want out. I'm sick of everything that goes on around here. I'm sick of the negative stuff, and you can take that upstairs to the fat man and tell him I said it." (1982)

LESSONS IN DISCIPLINE FROM THE CHAIRMAN

"Cliff Johnson came to camp twenty-five pounds too heavy. I had him doing wind sprints all day, every day."

AND WHILE CLIFF WAS RUNNING . . .

"Al [Rosen], we haven't been to the ice cream place for two nights."

AND WHILE CLIFF CONTINUED TO RUN

"The [ice cream] guy's gonna miss me."

CLIFF'S STILL OUT THERE

"I think I can use a banana split."

IT'S GETTING DARK, SIR

"My car drives itself to Baskin-Robbins. It can't help itself."

—on discipline . . . or important things you
discuss with your team president (1978)

◆ HOW ABOUT A PERSONAL TRAINER AND A PAIR OF TIGHTS?

"I'm the heavy. I don't like it, but I don't know how to change it."

George on Business

"Misunderstandings happen in business."

◆ HEY, BUSINESS IS BUSINESS

"I sold my egg company to my two sisters for three times what it was worth. They've never liked me since." (1992)

◆ HOLD OUT YOUR RICE BOWLS, FELLAS, IT'S FEEDING TIME

"For a long time, the partners put in and we were finally able to give them a decent payback."

> —defending a $100 million "payback" to the Yankees partnership in 1988. Fifty-five million personally went to Steinbrenner, the rest distributed among the team's seventeen other partners, including his wife, Joan.

◆ FAULTY TOWER

"When I was [banned], I left so much, we could have built a skyscraper with it."

> —on the financial condition of the Yankees upon his departure (1990)

◆ **WHAT'S MINE IS MINE, AND WHAT'S YOURS IS MINE**

"Why leave all that money? That's why you make investments, to make money."

> —defending a loan which used a Yankee
> television contract as collateral (1990)

◆ **THIS IS THE KIND OF FINANCIAL ACUMEN THE RUSSIANS DESPERATELY NEED**

"If you borrow at 7 or 7½ percent and invest at 10, you're smart."

> —economics made easy (1987)

◆ **THE CHECK'S IN THE MAIL**

"It's just a misunderstanding. Misunderstandings happen in business: they are not lies."

> —on problems with Yankee catcher
> Thurman Munson after he found out that
> Reggie Jackson was making more money
> (1977)

◆ SOUL, FAITH, HOPE, PRIDE, DIGNITY, BUT NOT A DIME

"I never wanted anyone to say, 'I went down a path with George Steinbrenner and lost money.'"

> —giving the devil his due, few have lost money in business dealings with Steinbrenner. And, in fact, he has often done the right thing when things have gone wrong. For example, when his first professional acquisition, the Cleveland Pipers basketball team, went belly-up, Steinbrenner—against the advice of lawyers who advised bankruptcy— managed to pay back all his investors all of their money. (1987)

◆ THINGS WE DON'T NEED TO KNOW DEPT.

"We start in our offices at 9:30. Why 9:30? I'll tell you why 9:30, people are fighting the traffic."

> —explaining benevolent management philosophy (1987)

◆ PARANOIA RUNS DEEP, INTO YOUR HEART IT CAN CREEP

"They say I was behind it when there was no money, and I'm behind it now that there is. They can't have it both ways. How come when the Mets or other teams spend all this money, nothing is made of it? But when we do it, we're the best team money can buy."

> —discussing the rising costs baseball owners must deal with (1987)

◆ EASY, EASY. OUR MISTAKE . . . WE THOUGHT YOU SAID "SHEEP"

"Are we cheap? We're adding another minor-league team next year. We have a manager and four full-time coaches at Columbus and a manager and two full-time coaches with every other minor-league team. How many teams have that? We fly only charters, never commercial flights. We stay at the best hotels and pay top dollar for that. Is that cheap?" (1987)

◆ A PRAGMATIC APPROACH TO CRITICISM IS ESSENTIAL TO GOOD BUSINESS PRACTICE

"Anything he says about me is water off a duck's back. Just keep those checks coming in."

> —responding to Fred Weinhaus, president and general manager of WABC radio, broadcaster of the Yankee games, who said, "We're paying fifty million over ten years for the rights [to broadcast]. We can't demand a pennant . . . we can demand a team that's competitive." (1990)

◆ THAT'LL KILL THIS DEAL

"You can't attach the exit of George Steinbrenner to it."

> —commenting on reports that Paramount Communications was interested in purchasing the Yankees (1991)

◆ UNLESS YOU CAN HIRE BETTER LAWYERS THAN THE OTHER GUY, IN WHICH CASE ALL BETS ARE OFF

"A cardinal rule in life is that when a man makes an agreement he sticks to it."

—to third baseman Graig Nettles (1977)

◆ "LIVE FROM YANKEE STADIUM— BASEBALLMANIA: THE NEW YORK YANKEES VS. SUPERSTARS OF THE WORLD WRESTLING FEDERATION IN A NO-HOLDS BARRED, TAG-TEAM EXTRAVAGANZA"

"Don't talk to me about aesthetics or tradition. Talk to me about what sells and what's good right now."

—proposing, in an interview, that a wild-card playoff format be adopted by baseball (1991)

◆ HELLSFIRE! THE MAN CALLS 'EM AS HE SEES 'EM

"The owners are partially to blame for the escalation in salaries—and you can probably say that the Yankees are among them."

—analyzing baseball's economic troubles (1991)

◆ EVER VIGILANT, EVER CONCERNED, THE BOSS LENDS A HELPING HAND TO A TROUBLED INDUSTRY

"You better get movies on Eastern, too."

> —while on a flight, advising an airline
> stewardess (1981)

◆ MY BASEBALL PEOPLE LET ME DOWN . . . AGAIN

"Definitely a mistake. He's the Cy Young winner. But who knew that five years ago?"

> —on pitcher Doug Drabek, whom the
> Yankees traded to the Pittsburgh Pirates in
> 1986 for pitcher Rick Rhoden

◆ FLIGHT OF THE GOOSE

"I think Goose was worried about the reaction of the fans, that he would be blamed for the firing of Billy [Martin]. He feels responsible for the change of managers because everybody knows how he feels about Billy."

> —blaming the loss of star relief pitcher
> Goose Gossage, who signed as a free
> agent with the Padres, on Gossage
> himself. The idea that Goose would be
> worried about anybody's reaction,
> particularly the fans, was widely
> dismissed. Gossage's explanation for
> bailing out after the 1983 season sounded
> more plausible: "A lot of the fun is taken
> out of the game here. I'm sick of that."

◆ BEEN GONE SO LONG LOOKS LIKE UP TO ME

"Well, you know, he eventually came back."

—on catcher Rick Cerone who, masochistically, returned to the Yankees twice. After Tour I (1980–84) he came back to play for The Boss in 1987 and 1990.

◆ SHORT-TERM MEMORY SKILLS DEPARTMENT

"I liked Jose. I can't remember who we traded for or how the trade was made."

—on pitcher Jose Rijo (1991)

◆ MR. STEINBRENNER, I'M JUST THE BATBOY AND I THINK THIS IS VERY UNFAIR

"You're the leader, you're the boss and you can't blame others. You must give directions." (1990)

◆ YOU'RE ON THE RECORD, BUT THE RECORD'S STUCK

"But I don't want to lay the blame on anyone else. I've made some bad decisions. I've made mistakes, I'm very demanding because I can't stand to see the Yankees anywhere but at the top." (1989)

◆ STUCK . . .

"I'm not easy to work for, but somebody has to be like that to keep us up there now we've made changes. This is the start of a new era." (1989)

◆ NOW HEAR THIS! ALL HANDS ON DECK!

"I used to be very hands-on, but lately I've been more hands-off, and I plan to become more hands-on and less hands-off and hope that hands-on will become better than hands-off, the way hands-on used to be." (1990)

George on Banishment

"Banned for life? I wasn't banned for life."

◆ GULP

"I'm anxious to come back, I really am."

*—January 1992, anticipating his return
from the permanently ineligible list to
actively running the New York Yankees on
March 1, 1993*

◆ AN OLD FOOTBALL MAN ZIGS AND ZAGS

"I want [the] Yanks back."

"My goal is not to run the team again."

"All I want to do is see the truth come out."

"It would be very difficult at my age, that's two years
. . . it would just be very difficult."

*—on the Spira case and its consequences
(1990)*

◆ SOME LIVES ARE SHORTER THAN OTHERS

"People keep coming up to me and asking, 'How
does it feel to be banned for life?' That's bullshit.
Banned for life. I wasn't banned for life." (1991)

◆ A LEADING EXPERT ON PREVARICATION ATTEMPTS TO CLEAR UP A SIMPLE MISUNDERSTANDING

"He also said that I can't even go to a ball game without his permission. That's a lie! The man lied!"

—*on baseball commissioner Fay Vincent's interpretation of the terms of his suspension from baseball (1991)*

◆ COMEUPPANCE WORK FOR YA?

"Let's not talk punishment."

—*responding to characterization of his baseball suspension (1991)*

◆ AND, OF COURSE, WE BELIEVE HIM

"I categorically deny ever talking to anyone with the Yankees about baseball."

—*in response to published reports in which unnamed Yankee officials are quoted as saying Steinbrenner violated terms of his banishment by conducting team business behind the scenes (1992)*

◆ BANG, BANG . . .

"We'll just take our shot in court."

—*seconds before he caved in and signed the banishment agreement with Fay Vincent*

◆ AND, BELIEVE IT OR NOT, HE'S JOKING

"Please judge me on my record in the past." (1990)

◆ **IN THE OLD DAYS, FOREVER WAS A LONG, LONG TIME**

"About how long is this going to last, Fay?"

> —on relinquishing his right to run the day-to-day operations

"How about forever?"

> —Fay Vincent, commissioner of baseball (1991)

◆ **BACK IN THE SADDLE AGAIN**

"At least I will have something to say about how they spend my money."

> —salvaging some dignity; Steinbrenner was allowed by Commissioner Vincent to deal with significant money matters having to do with the Yankees (1990)

◆ **PERHAPS I'VE HAD A CHANCE TO CONSIDER THE EFFECT I'VE HAD ON OTHER PEOPLE'S LIVES. PERHAPS NOT. PERHAPS IT WAS THEIR OWN DAMN FAULT.**

"Perhaps I've had a chance to step back."

> —musing on being out of baseball (1991)

◆ **AND MONKEYS FLY OUT OF OUR BUTTS**

"We sit at the Christmas table like two mummies."

> —on whether or not he talks baseball with his son-in-law, Joe Molloy, a Yankee vice-president, with whom Steinbrenner was banned from talking business (1991)

Vanity, Vanity, Thy Name Is Steinbrenner

"I am the Chief."

———————————

◆ COMPETITIVE STROLLING OR . . . "WE'RE KEEPING SCORE WHILE WE'RE KEEPING COMPANY"

"We used to go to P.J. Clarke's, and after dinner we'd walk down the street and see who got recognized more, me or her. I swear we went one-to-one."

—about Barbara Walters (1981)

◆ AND NOBODY'S HAD LESS FUN DOING IT

"Nobody has won as many games as we have in the past seventeen years." (1991)

◆ BETWEEN THE AQUA VELVA AND THE POLYESTER LEISURE SUIT, WE'RE TALKING A ROOMFUL OF POTENTIAL GROUPIES

"I'd like to be the first male reporter who tries to get into the women's tennis locker room." (1991)

◆ MOTHER TERESA. MOTHER HALE. MOTHER STEINBRENNER . . . MOTHER STEINBRENNER? MOTHER OF GOD!

"In the end, I'll put my good acts up against those of anybody in this country. Anybody." (1991)

◆ LET THE CHIPS FALL WHERE THEY MAY

"Last summer, for example, I gave ten thousand dollars that was needed to keep a playground running. At the time, I told them absolutely no publicity. But I've been taking so much lambasting lately that I don't care who knows now." (1991)

◆ IT AIN'T RIGHT! EARL WEAVER, DICK WILLIAMS, DAVEY JOHNSON . . . THESE GUYS ARE HOMELESS!

"One thing about me when I changed managers, though: I didn't let the people go; I didn't fire them and put them out in the street." (1991)

◆ IN FACT, I FOLLOWED THEM AROUND, BEGGING TO HELP

"I've never shut my door on anyone who needed me." (1979)

◆ **SOUNDS LIKE *OUR* KIND OF GUY**

"I don't enjoy a young guy off one good year who we plucked out of Toronto showing so little regard for me. It's not what I look for in my kind of guy."

> —*on losing Rick Cerone's arbitration case in 1981*

◆ **BUT BASEBALL WAS HIS DREAM, AND HE KNEW, EVEN THEN, THAT HE COULDN'T AFFORD TO SPREAD HIMSELF TOO THIN**

"I could sing better then he could."

> —*about songwriter Stephen Sondheim, with whom Steinbrenner says he sang in the Williams College Glee Club. Sondheim doesn't remember Steinbrenner. (1981)*

George on Family

*"Dad didn't give me an
allowance."*

◆ WHAT WITH THE DEBUTANTE BALLS AND ALL . . . THERE'S NO TIME ANYWAY

"I might not want my own daughter doing it."

—*on female journalists covering male sports*

◆ THEY'RE JUST SO VERY BITTER ABOUT HOW MY LIFE'S TURNED OUT

"I'm tired of my kids suffering."

—*on why he agreed to appear on Saturday Night Live in 1990; i.e., hoping to change the poor public perception of George M. Steinbrenner III*

◆ BRAINWASHING MIGHT WORK, OTHERWISE . . .

"I don't want them thinking that there wasn't at least as much good in their father's life as all the bad they've heard."

—*more on Saturday Night Live*

◆ WHO SAID THAT?

"Who said that?"

"Who said that?"

"Well, don't you ever say another goddamn thing about my daughter."

> —when George overheard a comment by Nettles on the team bus. Nettles had complained about having to play an exhibition game at his daughter's college.
> (1978)

◆ THE SEATS ARE UNCOMFORTABLE AND BALL PLAYERS SMELL

"Gene, I shouldn't have been on the bus."

> —apologizing to G. M. Michael for erupting at Graig Nettles on the team bus

◆ CALLING SUSAN AND JUDY! WE WANT YOU TO BUY SOMETHING!

"Dad didn't give me an allowance. He gave me chickens. I'd get my money through them. I'd get up early, clean the roosts, and then sell the eggs door to door. It was called the George Company. When I went away to school, I sold the company to my sisters, Susan and Judy. It became the S & J Company."

> —revealing early business sleight of hand
> (1992)

◆ WHAT ARE YOU TRYING TO SAY?

"He was a difficult perfectionist, in a way, who always sought excellence."

On his father

◆ THANKS A LOT, GEORGE, SR.

"I can't give enough credit to my dad. Anything I've ever accomplished I owe to him." (1978)

George and Lou Piniella

"He's practically like a son to me."

———————

◆ FATE WORSE THAN DEATH DEPARTMENT

"Don't worry. I'm really gonna fix him. I'm gonna make him manager."

—about Lou Piniella, to Barry Halper, a
limited partner in the Yankees (1985)

◆ SWEET LOU ALWAYS HAD IMPECCABLE INSTINCTS

"The simple fact is Piniella didn't even come back from lunch—if that was where he really was—to get a call from his boss at two o'clock."

—statement after Piniella missed a phone
call from The Boss (1986)

◆ JUST WONDERING . . . DOES POLYESTER BURN?

"I'm glad to see the players so firmly behind Lou Piniella. If this is their idea of support, then I'm happy not to have it."

—after the players burned a Steinbrenner
statement critical of manager Piniella
(1987)

◆ OR BETTER YET, SEATTLE—A RELATIVELY SAFE 3,000 MILES AWAY

"I know Lou still wants to manage. But he's too smart for that. Managing's an awful job, and Lou's above it. He belongs in the front office."

—*after Piniella's firing (1987)*

◆ AND HOLY COW, WHAT A SURPRISE THAT THEY PICKED YOUR FAVORITE GUY, LOU PINIELLA!

"They will have absolutely no stipulations or input from me."

—*announcing that Clyde King, his general manager, and Woody Woodward, his assistant, would decide the Yankee manager for 1986*

◆ AND YOU'VE GOT TO MUCK OUT THE DUGOUT, STRAIGHTEN UP YOUR LOCKER, ORGANIZE THE BATTING HELMETS, OH, AND LOU . . . SEE ME WHEN YOU'RE FINISHED

"Goddamn it, Lou, don't tell me you were out playing golf all day! I didn't send you to these meetings to play golf. I'll tell you this: Next year you're not going."

—*to Lou Piniella, whom he couldn't contact during baseball's winter meetings in 1987*

◆ HE JUST HAS AN UNCANNY RESEMBLANCE TO WAYNE NEWTON

"George Steinbrenner never implicated Lou Piniella as a gambler, other than a guy betting on horses at the track, like I do and like a lot of other fine people do."

—expressing regret that Piniella's name
was linked to the Spira case (1990)

◆ NUKE 'EM TILL THEY GLOW, BRO

"In the end, I'll win. I always do."

—during a dispute with manager Lou
Piniella, 1986. One thing he didn't win
was a tabloid reader poll. The question:
Do you back The Boss or Lou Piniella?
The results: 6,281 votes for Piniella
447 for Steinbrenner

A PHILOSOPHICAL INQUIRY

IN WHICH OWNER STEINBRENNER AND MAN-
AGER PINIELLA STATE THEIR RESPECTIVE PHILOS-
OPHIES ON THE 1986 YANKEE SPRING TRAINING
CAMP

OWNER

"[Training camp is going to be run with a] football
mentality. In football, you didn't want to go home
once the season ended. You'd stay around and watch
films, work on techniques. I'd spend seven hours in
the film room. I brought in the [Yankees] coaches
three days a week this winter. They studied film on
every one of our players. This way the coaches all
come to spring training prepared. They've done the
work that they normally do for the first two weeks."

MANAGER

"This is not a football camp. It's a baseball camp."
(1986)

◆ IF THIS IS AN EXAMPLE OF TREATING SOMEONE LIKE A SON, IMAGINE THE LIFE OF HANK STEINBRENNER

"I've learned to live with Lou Piniella. I've learned
that at times he's just not the brightest guy in the
world." (1986)

George on Commissioners

*"There are things I would never
want to come out in public."*

———————

◆ JUST AS WELL, IT WOULD'VE BROKEN YOUR WIFE'S HEART

"Bowie [Kuhn] and I never really got along. He wasn't my kind of guy. We just never had a relationship." (1991)

◆ WAIT UNTIL DAWN, THEN USE WHITE VINEGAR AND RUB REALLY HARD

"He rode off into the sunset and left the tough stuff."

—on Peter Ueberroth, after he resigned as baseball commissioner (1989)

◆ I'M SORRY, MR. UEBERROTH SIR, I JUST COULDN'T HOLD IT

"I don't want to interfere with the World Series, but I just can't wait any longer."

—on the firing of Lou Piniella and the hiring of Billy Martin (fifth time). Ueberroth had asked him to wait until the Series was over to hold the press conference. (1987)

◆ ANYWAY, THE WILY COYOTE PAJAMAS ARE NOBODY'S BUSINESS BUT MY OWN

"That's as true as I can tell you. There are things in there I would never want to come out in public."

—to Fay Vincent, on the political implications of his 1974 conviction

◆ SO IS CHUCKLES THE CLOWN

"Maybe you are smarter than I am."

—to Fay Vincent (1990)

◆ ONE OF THESE TIMES I'M GONNA CATCH A BREAK

"The commissioner is doing what he has to do."

—about the infamous pine tar game in which George Brett hit a ninth inning two-run homer which pulled the Royals in front 5–4. Umpire Tim McClelland disallowed the home run due to excessive pine tar on the bat handle. American League president Lee MacPhail overruled his umpire. Steinbrenner, of course, protested and after a lengthy dispute the game was resumed three weeks later and the Yankees lost. (1983)

◆ THIS MULTIPLE-PERSONALITY THING IS REALLY GOING AROUND . . .

"Peter Ueberroth is the greatest thing since chocolate ice cream. I'm a Ueberroth man."

—*after Ueberroth reinstated Mickey Mantle and Willie Mays to baseball (1985)*

"Bart Giamatti is a man of substance and integrity— far more substance than Peter Ueberroth. Ueberroth is more show than substance. He's a master opportunist." (1989)

George and Howie Spira

"If it was stupidity on my part, then it was."

◆ THINK NIGHT LIGHT

"If they can get to the president and they can get to the pope, they can get to anybody. I wasn't quaking in my boots, but I was scared."

—on gambler Howard Spira's potential as a danger (1990)

◆ SEEMS TO US THIS STRATEGY DIDN'T WORK TOO HOT

"I wouldn't want him thinking he's threatening me or bothering me. Otherwise he'd never let up."

—on Spira's potential as a pain (1990)

◆ AND THE SECOND?

"The first payment to Spira was a gift out of the goodness of my heart."

—explaining a financial disbursement to Spira (1990)

◆ A LIFETIME KNEE-JERK REACTOR GETS RELIGION

"I'm not going to be a character judge."

—on Spira as a man and citizen (1990)

◆ 40 G's TO A GAMBLER . . . YEP, STUPID.

"If it was stupidity on my part, then it was. But I honest to God felt that I could help this young man to get his life straight."

—during his testimony to the commissioner about Spira, a great rehab candidate (1990)

◆ AND WHAT I TOLD DALLAS AND YOGI AND BILLY AND DICKIE AND LOU AND AH, THAT CLYDE GUY—OH, AND BOB, TOO—HAD NOTHING TO DO WITH WHY I CANNED THEIR BUTTS

"What I tell Howard Spira has nothing to do with the reasons I gave him the money."

—in testimony on Spira, who brings out the worst in people (1990)

George and Reggie Jackson

"I don't think you're a very good outfielder."

◆ TANKS FOR THE MEMORIES

"If that isn't tanking, I've never seen tanking."

> —about Reggie Jackson after he had a
> poor series against Baltimore (1978)

◆ "FAST! TELL THE DOORMAN 'NO VISITORS' AND GET MY PHONE UNLISTED!"

"If there's something wrong, I want to help him. When a guy's going good, when he's hitting .300, and he's cocky and he makes mistakes—which Reggie can do—that's when I'll whack his ass, physically, mentally, any way. But when things are going bad and he's trying hard, I'm not going to come down on him, I'm not knocking him, I won't be on his ass. Now, when he needs me, I'm there for him."

> —after ordering a slumping Jackson to get
> a physical. Not everyone thought the
> physical constituted being "there" for
> Jackson. For example, the New York Post's
> headline blared: "George's Ugliest
> Hour . . . Boss Twisted Knife as Reggie
> Crumbled." (1981)

◆ THE EVIL TWIN SYNDROME

"It was an outside situation that occurred. Somebody lied."

> —on why Jackson left the Yankees (1991)

◆ PREMATURE EVALUATION

"See, we knew he was through."

> —bad-mouthing Reggie Jackson in his first year with the California Angels and in an early season slump. Jackson went on to hit 39 homers with 101 RBI's in that season of 1982. After leaving the Yankees he hit 138 more home runs to reach his total of 563.

◆ ANYONE FOR A DIJON COUNT?

"There isn't enough mustard in the United States to cover him, but when the time came to deliver, he did."

> —about Jackson, at the press conference announcing his induction into the Hall of Fame in 1993

George and Billy Martin

*"If anyone says I've been on Billy's
butt, he's a liar."*

◆ OR WOULD YOU RATHER WAIT UNTIL WE LOSE A REGULAR-SEASON GAME?

"Do you want to get fired right now?"

> —to Billy Martin after a 1977 spring
> training loss to the Mets

◆ AND THE OWNER'S OVER THE TOP

"The team is out of control."

> —on Billy's 1977 Yankee team, which
> careened to the World Series
> championship

◆ BUT SOMMMMETIMES HE MAKES ME SOOOOO MAD . . .

"I am not out to get Billy Martin."

> —denying reports that Martin was about
> to be fired (1977)

◆ PLAY NICE, BOYS

"The next time you drive me to a wall I'll throw you over it."

*—threatening Billy, a statement that,
coming from others, commonly resulted in
hospital visits (1977)*

◆ HOPE SPRINGS ETERNAL

"I think if it can be turned around, he's the guy to do it."

—on the advent of Billy II, June 1979

◆ DIDN'T WE HEAR THIS ON *ANOTHER WORLD?*

"But there are things that happen in sports, in marriage, when it's just not right for two people to continue a relationship even though they remain friends. That's what happened with Billy and I."

*—why he fired Billy after Martin decked
marshmallow salesman Joseph Cooper in
a Minneapolis bar (1979)*

◆ STAND TUNED FOR ADDITIONAL NEW ERAS

"This is a new era for the third time around."

—about Billy Martin regime III (1983)

◆ I AM WHAT I YAM

"Billy understands what I want. Neatness, detailed organizational procedures."

—*rhapsodizing about the possibilities of a new start with Martin (1983)*

◆ SO I UNCHAINED HIM FROM THE WATER COOLER ... AND TETHERED HIM OUT IN THE BULLPEN

"He was getting a little tired of the dugout."

—*on the demise of Billy III, December 1983*

◆ BUT STYLES CHANGE, AND IN THIS CASE, QUICKLY

"I can't criticize Billy's style and personality; in many ways it's a lot like mine. But Yogi's style is a factor in this. It may be the right style for 1984."

—*on firing Billy and hiring Yogi Berra (1983)*

◆ AND HE DID. ALMOST AS FAST AS YOU REMOVED THEM

"Billy is one of the few managers who can put fannies in the seats."

—*commenting on Martin's crowd-drawing ability (1979)*

◆ SAINT GEORGE PONDERS THE LARGER QUESTIONS

"I would be a very selfish guy if I let something like what happened stand in the way of Billy having a chance to improve his life. We're not just talking about baseball. We're talking about something a lot bigger than that. In this picture baseball is a poor third."

—*on Billy's troubles (1988)*

◆ WHAT'D YOU KNOW ABOUT RULES?

"He is a win-at-all-costs-within-the-rules kind of guy."

—*artfully describing Billy Martin (1977)*

◆ BUT THE HELL WITH IT . . . YOU'RE FIRED

"I'm not going to deal with the manager thing right now."

—*commenting on manager Martin's future at the end of the 1983 season. Billy III ended soon thereafter, and Yogi Berra was named manager for the 1984 season.*

◆ BULLY BALL

"I stayed away from this team, that was part of my agreement with Billy, part of what I said would be done and you didn't hear me talking about my players, my manager. Billy wanted this team and he has this team."

—about the 1983 season during which Steinbrenner was suspended for criticizing umpires, embroiled in the George Brett pine-tar incident, and fired a couple of pitching coaches for good measure

◆ EXCEPT THAT ONE TIME HE CAME INTO MY OFFICE WITH A FREDDY KREUGER MASK . . .

"There's a bond between Billy and me. We fight. We argue. I don't scare him, and he doesn't scare me."

—on the dawning of Billy V, 1987

◆ ANOTHER EPISODE OF "AS THE CLUBHOUSE TURNS"

"I'm convinced after speaking to various individuals that Billy Martin was victimized in this incident. Billy is my manager. Case closed."

—after yet another Martin bar altercation—this time at a Dallas topless joint called "Lace" in 1988

◆ **WELL, HE WAS KNEE-WALKING SLOSHED AND IT WAS AN ALTERCATION IN A GIN MILL AND, NO, IT WASN'T A FIRST-TIME SITUATION, BUT IT SURE IS SWELL TO HAVE AN UNDERSTANDING BOSS . . .**

"I find no fault with Billy over what happened to him. I find fault over where he was."

> —after the "Disgrace at Lace" incident in which Martin was badly beaten by a bouncer. "Where" he was, of course, was a topless bar—at 1:30 in the morning.

◆ **THEIRS IS NOT TO REASON WHY, THEIRS IS BUT TO DO AND DIE.**

"It is not the players' bleeping business what I do with this team."

> —During the volatile 1988 season in which Billy Martin was fired, following his Lace beating, Lou Piniella quit as general manager and was later hired as manager (and fired again at the end of the season), three pitching coaches were hired and fired, and the Yankees finished fifth.

◆ **AND REGULARLY TRASHING HIM ALMOST BROKE MY HEART**

"I loved Billy." (1991)

◆ **AND I'D LIKE TO GO ON RECORD AS SAYING THAT GEORGE STEINBRENNER IS ONE OF THE FINEST HUMAN BEINGS I'VE EVER HAD THE PLEASURE OF KNOWING, AND WORKING FOR HIM ALL THESE DIFFERENT TIMES HAS BEEN SOME OF THE BEST AND REWARDING EXPERIENCES OF MY PERSONAL AND PROFESSIONAL LIFE AND I'M NOT JUST SAYING THIS BECAUSE OF ANY POTENTIAL FOR FUTURE FINANCIAL GAIN ON MY PART. OK?**

"I've got to be careful what I say about George. I need the money."

—*Billy Martin on Steinbrenner (1988)*

George on Umpires

"The fine will be paid."

◆ NOPE

"We don't pay them enough to start with and we don't train 'em. They get trained at independent schools, which we have no control over. You know what they tell them there? They tell them not to take any guff from ball players, and if they give them any just get even with them next time. Can you believe that?"

—on the education of umpires (1980)

◆ ANYWAY, I DIDN'T KNOW IT WAS LOADED

"But I was hot. I wanted to win, but even my mother scolded me for it."

—on an incident in which an enraged George was captured on television cursing a stationary target—an umpire

◆ IN THE HEAT OF BATTLE, DUDE

"You f***ing homer."

—after National League umpire Lee Weyer made a call against the Yankees in a 1983 spring training game. Steinbrenner was fined $50,000 for the remarks.

◆ BUT THE AMERICAN LEAGUE WILL ALWAYS GIVE THE CLOSE PLAY TO THE PLAYER WHO RIGHTFULLY DESERVES IT

"The National League will always give the close play to the National League."

> —*about the supposed prejudice of National League umpires (1983)*

◆ THE BULL HORN JUST HAPPENED TO BE ON

"I was speaking privately to a friend."

> —*explaining why the dreaded press shouldn't have printed his intemperate umpire remarks (1983)*

◆ THE WALLS HAVE EARS, BABE

"It's a shame that any young writer would take my statement out of context just to get a sensational story."

> —*about Mike McAlary, now a New York Daily News columnist, who reported Steinbrenner's remarks (1983)*

◆ MR. INTEGRITY SPEAKS

"Bowie is very big on the integrity of the game, and this goes right to the heart of the integrity of the game."

> —*on Kuhn's $50,000 fine for George's 1983 comments to ump Lee Weyer*

◆ OF COURSE, WE DIDN'T THINK THAT. WHERE'S THE CHECK?

"I personally regret if in the reporting of the story the impression was given that I was questioning the integrity of National League president Chub Feeney or the umpires as a group. I was not and certainly apologize to them if that was their impression. The fine will be paid."

—Caving in, April 1983

◆ AND THE FANS ARE DAMNED LUCKY WE LET 'EM WATCH

"The umpires don't own the game, the owners own the game."

—after Billy Martin's suspension in a dirt-kicking incident with ump Dale Scott (1988)

George and Dick Howser

"I'd rather leave it this way, Stick."

—Dick Howser refusing an offer (from
Yankee general manager Gene Michael)
to keep his managing job after the
Yankees had fired him (1980)

DICK AND GEORGE

A VERY, VERY SHORT FILM BASED ON A REAL EX-
CHANGE BETWEEN A BASEBALL TEAM OWNER AND
HIS THIRD-BASE COACH

FADE IN:

EXT. BASEBALL FIELD - DAY

A runner is thrown out. The third-base coach may
have made a mistake. Maybe not.

INT. OWNER'S BOX—STADIUM - DAY

GEORGE, the florid, heavyset owner, stands up. Leans
out of the box. He's mad. He's really mad.

> GEORGE
> (*shrieks*)
> "Wake up down there at third base!"

DICK, the handsome third-base coach, looks up. Strides heroically into the dugout.

> DICK
> (*over his shoulder*)
>
> "Go to hell."

CLOSE UP George.

> GEORGE
> (*to camera*)
>
> "I filed that away. Those are the kind of things I remember."

FADE OUT (1980)

◆ PLUS, HE'S SNAPPY IN PINSTRIPES

"I don't care if he looks like a male model or a kewpie doll. He's tough enough for the job."

> —commenting on newly hired manager
> *Dick Howser* (1979)

◆ **AND NOW I'VE GOT AN UPSET STOMACH AND CAN'T FINISH MY CHOCOLATE ICE CREAM, WHICH MAKES ME EVEN MORE VERY UPSET AND EVEN MORE VERY DISAPPOINTED, BUT I LIKE DICK, I REALLY DO, AND, JUST BETWEEN YOU AND ME, I WON'T FIRE HIM UNTIL TOMORROW**

"I don't appreciate Dick Howser popping off like this. Howser I can't figure out. I'm very upset. I'm very disappointed in him."

—after Yankee manager Howser had quietly protested Steinbrenner's offering the third-base coaching job to Don Zimmer without informing him (1980)

◆ **YOU HAVE TO. HE'S GOT IT IN WRITING**

"Why am I paying the guy $500,000?"

—when Howser refused to put relief pitcher Goose Gossage in during a 1980 game

◆ **THEY WERE AROUND THE CORNER GETTING A PACK OF BUTTS**

"My players didn't lose this one."

—criticizing Howser's 1980 managerial strategy

◆ **SELECTED EXCERPTS FROM DICK HOWSER'S
FINAL PRESS CONFERENCE IN WHICH
PRINCIPAL OWNER GEORGE M. STEINBRENNER
III ANNOUNCED THAT MR. HOWSER HAD
RESIGNED AS NEW YORK YANKEE MANAGER**

"Were you fired?"

—*the press to Howser*

"I'm not going to comment on that."

—*Howser to the press (1980)*

◆ **BUT DON'T LET IT HIT YOU ON THE BUTT ON
THE WAY OUT**

"All of the discussions that have taken place were to
make sure that he was making the decision that he
really wanted to make. The door was open for his
return."

—*on Dick Howser's non-firing firing (1980)*

George and Yogi

"Yogi's a winner."

◆ AND HE'S GOT THE FINGERPRINTS TO PROVE IT

"If those players with the crocodile tears want to point a finger, let them point a finger at themselves. They're the ones who fired Yogi."

—*on Yogi Berra's firing (1985)*

◆ GEEZ, THINGS SURE CAN CHANGE FAST IN THIS CRAZY WORLD

"Yogi will be the manager this year, period. A bad start will not affect Yogi's status, either."

—*on Yogi Berra's job security, February 1985. Berra was fired in April.*

◆ UNLIKE SWINE FLU, THERE'S NO SHOT THAT'LL PROTECT YOU FROM THE BOSS

"Who's Yogi? He's not immune. The bottom line is winning."

—*Berra gets the ax (1985)*

◆ I BELIEVED IT WHEN I SAID IT. HONEST TO GOD

"Yogi's willing to take the challenge. Yogi's a winner."

—poor Yogi. On his hiring as manager
(1983)

◆ AN' I AIN'T GONNA, NEITHER

"That's why we created that special day for catchers. We wanted him to come back. But he didn't."

—trying to entice Yogi Berra back to
Yankee Stadium six years after he was
fired, 1991. Berra pledged that he
wouldn't return while Steinbrenner owned
the team.

George and Dallas Green

"I've got absolute faith in Dallas."

◆ IF ONLY LIFE WAS SO SIMPLE

"Every year we've gone in feeling confident and we haven't won out. This year I don't feel so confident, so maybe we'll win. It depends on the job Dallas Green does."

—before the 1989 season

◆ JUST A COUPLE OF LITTLE TEENY-WEENY ADJUSTMENTS AND I'M OUTA HERE

"I told Dallas, 'Let me indulge myself a little on this one.' "

—on insisting that aging veterans Tommy John and Ron Guidry be invited to spring training against his manager's wishes. "It's your team Dallas," Steinbrenner said, "but I've got just a couple of things." (1989)

◆ DO IT AGAIN, DALLAS. QUICK, CLYDE, THE PELLET GUN!

"I love it when the manager says, 'We stink.' . . . We haven't had managers stand up like that."

—after Green had criticized the Yankees' play (May 1989)

◆ BUT YOU GO 56–65 AND YOU'RE HISTORY, DALLAS

"I know that some people will say this is usually the kiss of death from me, but it isn't. I'm not alarmed. I'm not panicking. I've got absolute faith in Dallas and Syd [Thrift, new Yankee GM]."

> —When Green heard his quote he responded: "If I go 1–161, I'm still in here?" (1989)

◆ IT'S NOT SCHOOL WE HATE, IT'S THE PRINCIPAL OF THE THING

"Certain things he does sometimes make me feel like I'm the principal of the school in the movie *Hoosiers*. The principal says, 'I wish I could understand why you're doing these things.' And the coach, Gene Hackman, says, 'Believe me, I know what I'm doing.' I hope he's right."

> —about manager Green in June 1989

◆ WE FEEL THIS STATEMENT IS A FELONY IN AND OF ITSELF AND WILL SAY NO MORE. LET'S MOVE ON

"The only other time I reacted to him was when he was quoted in *Sports Illustrated* last week saying, 'You never know with that guy.' I sent him a little note with the clipping, saying, 'I don't recall ever calling my boss "that guy." ' I think the public knows that he knows I care what he says just as he cares what I say."

> —comment on his public disagreement with Green (1989)

◆ BUT HE DAMN WELL BETTER BE LISTENING

"I will have no more to do with it at this point. He won't hear another word from me."

—*about Green, as the Yankee 1989 season continues poorly*

◆ MY TRIGGER FINGER'S GITTIN' ITCHY, THOUGH

"I don't know. I can't answer that. It's the manager's job and I don't intend to interfere. I've made one or two suggestions, but I've said from the beginning that I'd stay out of the way and I've kept that promise."

—*And it goes from bad to worse (1989)*

◆ INTERFERENCE RUNS DEEP, INTO YOUR HEART IT WILL CREEP

"I never said we should win it, I said I felt we should be close to it. But his team has not jelled. It has not come together."

—*Without Dave Winfield, lost for the season with a back injury, and Ricky Henderson, traded after criticizing teammates, the 1989 Yankees went through a team-record fifty players en route to their worst record since 1967.*

◆ AND IF THEY DO, THEY'RE FIRED

"This year, no one can say I interfered."

> —After the 1989 season. During the year Steinbrenner fired manager Green and forced out GM Syd Thrift, talked about bringing back Billy Martin (for Billy VI) and Lou Piniella (III), and considered hiring Dick Williams.

◆ OKAY, IGOR, BRING DALLAS OUT OF THE CELLAR NOW AND LET'S SEE WHAT HE HAS TO SAY

"But I'm not that kind of guy. I wouldn't do that to Dallas or anyone else. I told him I would pay him and the coaches in full. He said, and I quote directly, 'I know you're that kind of guy, George, and that's why I respect you so much.' That is exactly what he said. He doesn't dare deny it."

> —commenting on a dispute with his fired manager (1989)

◆ AND TO ALL A GOOD NIGHT . . .

"Well, will you stay on? I'll make it worth your while."

> —moments after firing Green. The ex-manager rejected the idea, responding: "This experience is something I have to get over." (1989)

George and Dave Winfield

"Mr. May"

◆ FOR EXAMPLE, HE COULD POINT TO THE OWNER'S BOX AND SAY, 'BE LIKE HIM.'

"I really think David felt that what he does for youth could be done better from Yankee Stadium."

—commenting, in January 1981, on
Winfield's decision to move to the Yankees
for the coming season

◆ MALICE CLASSICO

"Where's Reggie Jackson? We need a Mr. September or a Mr. October. Winfield is Mr. May." (1985)

◆ AND IF I HAD ONE OF THOSE REALLY NEAT OUTFITS WITH THE FRINGE, AND THE SPURS AND THE SIX-SHOOTERS. WOW, THAT'D REALLY BE COOL!

"[Angels owner] Gene Autry overwhelmed him with that offer. If I had a horse named Champion and a guitar like the Cowboy, and had made all those old movies, then maybe I could afford that kind of contract for him."

—Commenting on the California Angels'
contract offer to Dave Winfield (1990)

◆ AND THEN THE PRINCIPAL OWNER LIT A CAMEL, TURNED UP THE COLLAR OF HIS TRENCHCOAT, AND DISAPPEARED INTO THE SHADOWS OF THE CITY

"I think we're beginning to see the unraveling of what has been a very carefully plotted PR campaign concerning Dave Winfield over the years."

> —about Winfield's public image, which had been damaged over a disagreement with Willie Randolph. The unraveling never reached the fans, who in the Steinbrenner-Winfield tiff chose Winfield, by all accounts cheering far more for the player in 1988 than ever before.

◆ GET HIM THE FIVE-POUND NO-DOZE BOX

"The man has been inspired. . . . It's not an answer to George Steinbrenner. I think he's trying to show his teammates that maybe he shouldn't have written the book when he did and shouldn't have written what he did about them. . . . But I hope [Winfield] doesn't go to bed on us in August or September." (1988)

◆ AND THEN DUCK . . .

"George Steinbrenner will have no part in making a decision about Dave Winfield. The other two fellows [general manager Lou Piniella and manager Billy Martin] are taking care of that. I am not involved and will not be involved. I've told them that when they make a decision to let me know about it."

—as a contretemps over Winfield's book pointed to the slugger being traded (1988)

◆ OR MAYBE ANOTHER TEAM? SAY, TORONTO

"If you can't produce a lot of RBI's with [Rickey] Henderson, [Willie] Randolph, and [Don] Mattingly batting ahead of you, you might as well try another sport."

—commenting in July on Winfield, who ended up with 104 RBI's for the 1986 season

◆ AHH . . . SHUT UP!

"[If Winfield] is quoted accurately that I have been responsible for the fact that [manager] Lou Piniella has seen fit to bench him against right-handed pitchers, he is off base. Now, if he were to say that I fully support the move to bench him vs. right-handed pitchers at this time, he would be absolutely accurate. And if he now says, following his public outburst yesterday, that I am responsible from this one point, he may very well be accurate."

—commenting on Winfield, who described his series of benchings as "stupid" and "ignorant" (1986)

◆ GOOD IDEAS ARE ALWAYS MINE, BAD IDEAS ARE ALWAYS YOURS

"I told Lou and Woody Woodward that if [Winfield] really wants to hit cleanup so badly, then put him there and find out what he's made of. We might as well put the monkey on his back. Well, he was more than outstanding. He was unbelievable." (1987)

◆ TELL IT TO THE ATLANTA BRAVES, 1992

"Dave Winfield just isn't the winner Reggie Jackson was. Does anyone know where I can find Reggie Jackson? I let Mr. October get away and I got Mr. May, Dave Winfield." (1985)

◆ LIKE, SAY, NINTH INNING, FINAL GAME, 1992 WORLD SERIES?

"He gets his numbers when they don't count."

—criticizing the timing of Dave Winfield's offensive production. This after Winfield had four consecutive years of 100 plus RBI's for the Yankees (1988)

◆ SIX YEARS WRONG AND COUNTING . . .

"[Winfield] is not the player he used to be." (1986)

◆ OTHER THAN TRIVIAL THINGS LIKE WORLD SERIES VICTORIES

"There is not that much out there for Dave at his age."

—on Winfield in 1989

◆ BUT THE POLICE FORCE FED US COFFEE AND SUGAR PRODUCTS AND, WELL, WE WERE HYPER AS HELL AND RAPPED THE NIGHT AWAY . . .

"I wish that my people and myself would be allowed to shut up and that Winfield and his people would shut up."

—about the dispute with the Winfield Foundation (1989)

◆ NOT TO MENTION CASPAR

"Winfield doesn't want to play center field because he's scared of the ghost of Joe DiMaggio." (1988)

◆ DAVID . . . WINFIELD?

"I'm genuinely happy for David."

—after the 1992 World Series

The Principal Owner's Epiphany

Late one summer night, the Principal Owner, alone as usual, was sitting quietly on his pitcher's mound in his large, metropolitan baseball stadium with a quart of Rocky Road and a genuine Yankee Spoon Day spoon when storm clouds gathered overhead, streaks of lightning split the night sky, thunder boomed, and rain began to fall. Instinctively, the Principal Owner protected his Rocky Road. A movement in the dugout caught his attention. He shielded his eyes with a subpoena he happened to be carrying in his coat pocket and peered through the downpour. Ghostly figures wearing pinstripes floated eerily near the battered water cooler, giving bunt, take, and steal signs to a team who was not there. The sounds of games past, and games yet to be played, echoed through the empty ball orchard. Mesmerized, the Principal Owner rose to his feet and moved toward the strange but wonderful scene before him.

A tremendous bolt of lightning coursed through the magnificent city-owned structure and plunged into the fabled Yankee team enclosure. The ghostly pinstriped shapes disappeared, leaving only charred Yankee baseball caps and tattered lineup cards in their place. The rain stopped. A shaft of moonlight pierced the clouds and enveloped the Principal Owner in its golden glow. His eyes followed the beam of light up to the heavens and there, improbably, was Casey Stengel holding many Yankee jerseys and wearing a frown. The Principal Owner sensed that Casey was upset.

As suddenly as it came, the vision was gone, and the stadium was as it was before.

The Principal Owner waddled back to his pitcher's mound and the Rocky Road. As he reached down for his Yankee spoon he was struck with a blinding revelation and the meaning of the vision became crystal clear:

"I probably shouldn't have changed managers as much as I did." (1991)

Volleys and Thunder:
Others on George

"Everything you've heard about George Steinbrenner is true. That's the problem."

—Dave Winfield

"He's a direct, mean man. He has no feelings for other people."

> —*Pearl Davis, a Yankee secretary for ten years*

"It was a beautiful thing to behold with all thirty-six oars working in unison."

> —*Jack Buck, Cardinal announcer, joking about the Boss's new yacht*

"Steinbrenner won't let anyone relax. It's what I call his corporate mentality. He throws fear into everybody. He makes the players fear for their jobs. That's his theory and it works. But it's not a pleasant way to have to play."

> —*Tony Kubek, Yankee announcer*

"The more we lose, the more often Steinbrenner will fly in. And the more he flies in, the better the chance there'll be a plane crash."

> —*Graig Nettles, Yankee third baseman (1977)*

"I tell George what I think and then I do what he says."

— *Bob Lemon, Yankee manager (1982)*

"The sweetest words to George are 'Yes, Boss.'"

— *Graig Nettles (1978)*

"Winning isn't fun for George. Nothing is fun for George. He takes everything so seriously."

— *Marty Appel, former Yankee p.r. director*

"George Steinbrenner talks out of both sides of his wallet."

— *Ron Luciano, former umpire*

"A liar . . . a tyrant . . . a graceless lout . . . a statesman in the Alexander Haig mold."

— *Mike Lupica*

"[George Steinbrenner] is like a *Titanic* in search of an iceberg."

— *Bowie Kuhn*

"It's the first smart thing he's ever done."

— *Henry Steinbrenner, George's father, on his son's purchase of the Yankees*

"I'm the first guy he sees after getting bad news."

— *John Sibayan, George's longtime chauffeur, explaining why he has been fired more times than he can remember, "only to be hired back before he can turn off the car" (1990)*

"George buys off pain."

—*Dick Schaap*

"I see Steinbrenner, unregistered egomaniac and all-time second-guesser, firing his team and playing all nine positions himself."

—*Ray Fitzgerald*

"How do you know when George Steinbrenner is lying? When his lips are moving."

—*Jerry Reinsdorf, at 1983 All-Star game party*

"In every other job I've had with him, he seemed to respect my opinion to some degree. But when you become his manager, it's like your IQ drops by fifty percent. All of a sudden you don't know anything."

—*Gene Michael (1981)*

"He really should stick to horses. At least he can shoot them if they spit the bit."

—*Reggie Jackson (1982)*

"It is apparent to me that Mr. Steinbrenner does not appreciate the gravity of his conduct."

—*Fay Vincent*

"I sat through the two days of Mr. Steinbrenner's testimony, and I am able to judge the degree of candor and contrition present in this case."

—*Fay Vincent*

"An owner of a major league baseball club may not pay a gambler for information intended to be used in a dispute involving the owner and a ballplayer."

> —Fay Vincent, "Summary of Decision"
> that put Steinbrenner on the permanently
> ineligible list

"I couldn't think of anyone other than Saddam Hussein I'd rather have making these complaints."

> —Fay Vincent, commenting on statements
> by Steinbrenner complaining that he'd
> been treated unfairly during investigation
> leading to his resignation

"I like George, but if I had to describe him in one quick sentence it would be: 'If something is wrong, it has to be someone else's fault.' "

> —Edward Bennett Williams, owner,
> Baltimore Orioles

"The Yankee fans deserve a new chapter. This one has come to an end."

> —Dave Winfield, commenting on
> Steinbrenner's "permanent" ban from
> baseball

"Not for the first time, I didn't believe him."

> —Dick Schaap, after a conversation
> with George

"He likes to have power over people. He lies. He lies for practice."

> —Dick Schaap

"One of his major drives in life is to manipulate people. He enjoys having control over their lives. You can almost see invisible strings on the people that work for George. He likes to have and exercise power. But the way he yells at secretaries and employees, that's just cruel."

—Dick Schaap

"My advice to him would be to have a strong stomach and a long contract."

—Dick Howser, after being fired, to Gene Michael, his replacement as Yankee manager (1980)

"I tell you it hasn't been easy, that's for sure."

—Lou Piniella, while Yankee manager

"George calls me his friend? With friends like that, who needs enemies?"

—Lou Piniella

"He's a sap for children. He's a sap for family. He's a sap for good causes. He's patriotic. He'd make a fine king, and I don't think he'd disagree with that."

—Tom McEwen, sports editor and a close friend

"George M. Steinbrenner III was born on the Fourth of July, which seems appropriate, but he would have preferred December 25."

—Tom McEwen, joking

"I worked for the FBI for thirty years. J. Edgar Hoover was a tough boss, but he was fair. Steinbrenner is another Hoover. He's a tough man to work for, but he's fair."

—*Phil McNiff, a former FBI supervisor,*
now a Steinbrenner employee

"George is the neighborhood bully."

—*Tony Kubek*

"There is nothing so limited as a limited partner of George Steinbrenner."

—*John McMullen, upon selling his stock*
in the Yankees (1973)

A conversational snippet between Clyde King, Yankee executive, and Hank Steinbrenner, George's son.

KING: "What do you think would really help this team?"
HANK: "Get rid of my father." (1990)

"You come here and you play and you get no respect. They treat you like shit. They belittle your performance and make you look bad in the media. After they give you the money, it doesn't matter. They can do whatever they want. They think money is respect."

—*Don Mattingly, criticizing Steinbrenner*
(1988)

"This isn't my f**king team, it's your f**king team! You make all the f**king decisions. You make all the f**king moves. You get all the f**king players that nobody else wants. You put this f**king team together, and then you just sit back and wait for us to lose so you can blame everybody else because you're a f**king chicken-shit liar."

—Yogi Berra in 1984 after mounting Steinbrenner criticism

"George doesn't know a f**king thing about the game of baseball. That's the bottom line. When you've got a guy who wants total control and he doesn't know my job or the strengths and weaknesses of his ball club, you've got a big problem."

—Dallas Green after being fired by Steinbrenner (1989)

"Once you leave the Yankees, once you recover from the shock and start feeling like your old self again, you realize that anything you do from that point on in your life is never going to be as difficult."

—Dave Collins, Yankee outfielder (1982)

"You gotta be kidding!"

—Whitey Herzog, when asked about a rumor he might someday work for George Steinbrenner

"Your comments and threats that 'I had made an enemy for life' . . . 'Keep looking over your shoulder because I'll be after you' . . . 'I'll get you no matter how long it takes' . . . 'I want to hurt you.' etc., were those you might expect from a gangster hit man rather than from a principal owner of a major league baseball club."

—Bill Murray, Bowie Kuhn's top administrative aide, in a letter to Steinbrenner dated April 5, 1981, in response to Steinbrenner's phone call to him. (The two clashed when the commissioner's office nixed a complex trade between the Pittsburgh Pirates, the California Angels, and the Yankees.)

"We looked into it and there's nothing to it."

—Fay Vincent, responding to Steinbrenner's assertion that one of the reasons he gave money to Howard Spira was that he feared he would reveal information on the gambling habits of Lou Piniella

"Steinbrenner is a bumbling idiot. He is a disgrace to sports, and you can quote me."

—Tom Weisel, chairman, U.S. Ski Racing Federation

"As long as you keep in mind that it's the owner first, the club second, and the players third, you don't have any problems."

—unidentified Yankee (1987)

"His recollections don't conform with objective reality."

> —Edward Bennett Williams, Steinbrenner's
> own attorney, being quoted by David
> Greenfield, an attorney representing
> Howard Spira

"On the other side of the wall—where the trash dumpster is."

> —Dave Winfield answering a question
> from Mike Lupica about where
> Steinbrenner would someday put his
> monument at Yankee Stadium

"It's a good thing Babe Ruth isn't still here. If he was, George would have him bat seventh and tell him he's overweight."

> —Graig Nettles (1986)

"He was 0—8—1 . I want to know how he got the tie."

> —Billy Martin, on Steinbrenner's one-year
> stint as an assistant football coach at
> Northwestern

"What does George know about Yankee pride? When did he ever play for the Yankees?"

> —Billy Martin and Peter Golenbock,
> Number 1

"George is an overbearing, arrogant, arbitrary, authoritarian son of a bitch. There's no denying that. But I just love him. We all do. You ask yourself why he can't be more like everybody else. Well, if he was, he wouldn't be George Steinbrenner."

—Pete Smythe, an old friend

"I don't know if he was good for baseball, but I think his being kicked out of baseball—if that's what really happened—is really bad for American business and human relations because we have now lost a symbol of how not to do things."

—Jim Bouton, former Yankee pitcher and co-author of the best-selling Ball Four

"George took all the fun out of being an owner."

—Thomas Evans, one of Steinbrenner's original limited partners in the purchase of the Yankees in 1972

"Don't use my name. George might have my stadium pass revoked."

—a New York Yankee limited partner speaking to a Wall Street Journal reporter on condition of anonymity

"You lied, bullied, insulted, manipulated, and generally acted like a jerk."

—an open letter to Steinbrenner from John Cole, editor of the Lorain Journal, characterizing the negotiations with Steinbrenner's American Shipbuilding Company, which was located in Lorain. AmShip eventually moved to Tampa.

"[He called] with syrupy, sweet promises that he would do everything he could to keep jobs in Lorain. As usual with George Steinbrenner's promises, they soon turned to castor oil."

—*Senator Howard Metzenbaum of Ohio (1984)*

"I feel I was misled and double-crossed."

—*Representative Donald Pease of Ohio, about the Lorain negotiations*

"In the years the Steinbrenner group got into this [professional baseball], it was a real gravy train. Where else in American industry are employees depreciable?"

—*an IRS official commenting on sports franchises as tax shelters in 1970s*

"Let's go, Mets."

—*Aqueduct horse racing fans to Steinbrenner celebrating a victory at Wood Memorial in the Winner's Circle*

"George is a mouse studying to be a rat."

—*writer John Schulian*

"I've heard of phantom punches, but never phantom victims."

—*Edward Bennett Williams after George claimed to be in a fistfight with two Dodger fans in a elevator (1981)*

"Anyone can manage the New York Yankees. We have an abundance of talent. You just make up the lineup card and let us play."

—Willie Randolph on the Yankees managers' roulette game of the 1970s

"There's no reason for the players to panic, because Steinbrenner is panicking enough for everyone."

—anonymous player (1980)

"George Steinbrenner has never figured out that a baseball season is not a high-speed car chase."

—Peter Gammons, writer

"George is a man of his word, even though a lot of times you have to get it in writing to make sure of it."

—Catfish Hunter

Postscript

"There's a fine line between being colorful and being an asshole."

—Ted Turner, owner, Atlanta Braves (not
necessarily referring to George
Steinbrenner, but if the shoe fits . . .)

The Facts

The Managers' Merry-Go-Round

◆

Year	Manager	Record	AL East Pos.
1973	Ralph Houk	80–82	4th
1974	Bill Virdon	89–73	2nd
1975	Bill Virdon	53–51	
	Billy Martin	30–26	3rd
1976	Billy Martin	97–62	1st
1977	Billy Martin	100–62	1st
1978	Billy Martin	52–42	
	Dick Howser	0–1	
	Bob Lemon	48–20	1st
1979	Bob Lemon	34–30	
	Billy Martin	55–41	4th
1980	Dick Howser	103–59	1st
1981	Gene Michael	59–48	
	Bob Lemon	13–15	3rd
1982	Bob Lemon	6–8	
	Gene Michael	44–42	
	Clyde King	29–33	5th
1983	Billy Martin	91–71	3rd
1984	Yogi Berra	87–75	3rd
1985	Yogi Berra	6–10	
	Billy Martin	91–54	2nd
1986	Lou Pinella	90–72	2nd

Year	Manager	Record	AL East Pos.
1987	Lou Pinella	89–73	4th
1988	Billy Martin	40–28	
	Lou Pinella	45–48	5th
1989	Dallas Green	56–65	
	Bucky Dent	18–22	5th
1990	Bucky Dent	18–31	
	Stump Merrill	49–64	7th
1991	Stump Merrill	71–91	5th
1992	Buck Showalter	76–86	5th

Nightmare:
An Annotated Chronology of the Steinbrenner Years

◆

Jan. 3, 1973: The nightmare begins. A group headed by George Steinbrenner—who owns 20 percent—and former CBS executive Michael Burke purchases the Yankees from CBS for $10 million. A writer who attended Steinbrenner's first press conference later recalled, "My first impression was this guy's full of shit."

April 28, 1973: Putsch-y! Putsch-y! Steinbrenner forces Burke out as Yankee president, leaving George as top dog in the Yankee hierarchy. Though Burke, a Yankee official since 1966, remains a limited partner for a short time, the Steingrabber era has begun.

Sept. 30, 1973: *"Après moi, le deluge":* On the last day of the season, lifetime pinstriper Ralph Houk resigns as Yankee skipper.

Jan. 4, 1974: Bill Virdon is named manager of the Yankees for the 1974 season, after Steinbrenner's efforts at acquiring Dick Williams were rebuffed by Williams' boss, A's owner Charlie Finley.

April 15, 1974: Whoops! Fifteen-count indictment against Steinbrenner is handed up in Cleveland federal court for violations of election laws. Steinbrenner, the indictment charged, made illegal contributions to the Nixon campaign. Maximum penalties if convicted: 55 years in prison and $110,000 in fines.

April 19, 1974: Pleads not guilty to all 15 counts in federal indictment.

Aug. 23, 1974: Pleads guilty to one count of conspiracy to make illegal campaign contributions. The Boss is now a felon.

Aug. 30, 1974: Fined $15,000 by federal court. Pays in loose pennies.

Nov. 27, 1974: Suspended from baseball by commissioner Bowie Kuhn because of guilty plea. When ice cream privileges are also taken away, George breaks into tears.

Dec. 31, 1974: During his suspension, with the permission of the commissioner, Steinbrenner signs pitcher Catfish Hunter to record five-year contract worth $3.35 million.

Aug. 2, 1975: Billy I. Virdon is fired and replaced by Billy Martin. Gotham bartenders celebrate.

March 1, 1976: George's suspension from baseball lifted after 15 months because of a lifetime first: good behavior.

Nov. 29, 1976: Signs Reggie Jackson to a five-year contract. "As the Clubhouse Turns," a new soap opera, is announced by MSG Network.

July 24, 1978: Nine months after leading the Yankees to the world championship, Martin resigns as manager of the Yankees after being quoted saying about Jackson and Steinbrenner: "One's a born liar, the other's convicted." Some suggest alcohol may have been involved. Bob Lemon is named Martin's replacement.

July 29, 1978: On Old Timer's Day, Yankees announce that Martin will return as manager beginning the 1980 season.

June 18, 1979: Billy II. Bob Lemon is fired and replaced by Billy Martin.

Oct. 28, 1979: Steinbrenner announces that Martin will not be rehired for the 1980 season and that Dick Howser is the new Yankee manager.

Nov. 11, 1979: Bowie Kuhn fines Steinbrenner $5,000 for tampering with outfielder Brian Downing of the California Angels. Downing says Steinbrenner is a good kisser.

Nov. 31, 1980: Dick Howser resigns after winning 103 games—the most in baseball—and a division title. Gene Michael named new manager—hair turns gray.

Dec. 15, 1980: Steinbrenner signs Dave Winfield to a 10-year, $20 million contract and observes that the outfielder "sure is tall."

June 26, 1981: Bowie Kuhn reprimands Steinbrenner for tampering with free agent amateur Billy Cannon, Jr. Cannon says that it was "fun."

Sept. 6, 1981: Gene Michael fired after playful verbal skirmishes with Steinbrenner escalate. Michael later reports, "As soon as I said, 'Your momma wears combat boots,' I was a goner." Bob Lemon named new Yankee manager and claims to have "no opinion" on Mom Steinbrenner's footwear.

Oct. 20, 1981: Steinbrenner, sporting minor injuries, reports he was attacked in an elevator by two Dodger fans during World Series. Claims total victory in fisticuffs. No witnesses.

Oct. 25, 1981: Steinbrenner apologizes to Yankee fans for poor performance during World Series loss to Dodgers. Impressed with George's improving manners, fans say, "Thank you."

Jan. 22, 1982: Jackson signs $4 million contract with California Angels. Steinbrenner will later call letting Jackson go one of his biggest mistakes.

May 25, 1982: Winfield accuses Steinbrenner of defaulting on his ten-year obligation to donate $300,000 annually to the nonprofit Winfield Foundation.

Jan. 11, 1983: Billy III. Bartenders giddy.

April 19, 1983: Kuhn fines Steinbrenner $5,000 for questioning the integrity of National League umpires, particularly Lee Weyer.

May 31, 1983: Upon being suspended for one week by American League president Lee MacPhail for statements made questioning the integrity of umpires John Shulock and Derryl Cousins (whose work he called "a disgrace"), George breaks into downbeat rendition of the Coasters' "Why's Everybody Always Picking on Me."

July 3, 1983:   Fined $5,000 for remarks about Chicago co-owner Jerry Reinsdorf.

Dec. 16, 1983:   Martin is fired and replaced by Yogi Berra.

Dec. 23, 1983:   Yankees fined $250,000 by Bowie Kuhn and ordered to pay $50,000 in legal fees because of Steinbrenner's statements regarding the July 24 "pine tar" game.

April 28, 1985:   Billy IV. Yogi is fired, replaced by Billy Martin. Bartenders can't believe their good fortune.

Oct. 27, 1985:   Martin fired, replaced by Lou Piniella.

Oct. 19, 1987:   Billy V. Piniella moved "upstairs" to general manager as Martin is hired as Yankees manager.

Oct. 31, 1987:   Following months of dispute with New York City mayor's office and rumors that Yanks would relocate to New Jersey, Steinbrenner signs a 30-year lease in exchange for parking and security improvements around the stadium.

March 29, 1988:   Lou Piniella resigns as Yankees' general manager.

March 29, 1988:   *Winfield: A Player's Life* is released, blasting Steinbrenner. Steinbrenner puts Winfield on the trading block.

June 23, 1988:   Five and out: Martin fired. Piniella II begins.

Oct. 7, 1988:   Dallas Green hired as Yankee manager.

Jan. 6, 1989:   Winfield sues Steinbrenner.

Jan. 10, 1989:   Steinbrenner sues Winfield.

Jan. 19, 1989:   Ronald Reagan pardons Steinbrenner for his Nixon campaign contribution felony conviction. Church bells toll throughout the land, women and children weep.

Aug. 19, 1989:   Dallas Green fired. Bucky Dent named manager.

Sept. 6, 1989:   Steinbrenner and Winfield settle mutual lawsuits. Lawyers go into mourning.

Jan. 8, 1990:   Gambler Howie Spira receives two checks from Steinbrenner, totaling $40,000. Spira claims the money is for digging up dirt on Winfield. Steinbrenner initially says he gave the money to Spira "out of the goodness of my heart." Other explanations follow.

Jan. 26, 1990:   Steinbrenner asserts that Dent will be the team's manager for all of 1990. Dent's hair turns gray.

March 18, 1990:   *New York Daily News* breaks story of Steinbrenner's $40,000 payments to Spira.

March 23, 1990:   Spira arrested by FBI for extortion of Steinbrenner.

March 24, 1990:   At commissioner Fay Vincent's request, Washington lawyer John Dowd begins investigations of Spira-Steinbrenner relationship. Steinbrenner's hair turns gray.

May 11, 1990: Yanks trade Winfield to California Angels for pitcher Mike Witt. Citing his status as a 10-and-5 player Winfield refuses the trade. Eventually he relents and reports to Angels.

June 6, 1990: Bucky Dent fired. Carl "Stump" Merrill named manager. Merrill's remaining hairs turn gray.

June 7, 1990: Dowd submits his report to Vincent.

July 5, 1990: Vincent fines Steinbrenner a total of $225,000 for remarks harmful to the Angels' bargaining position with Winfield in the trade with the Angels.

July 6, 1990: Steinbrenner finishes two-day, 372-page testimony before commissioner Fay Vincent on the Spira-Winfield case.

July 30, 1990: Vincent orders Steinbrenner to resign as general managing partner of the New York Yankees by Aug. 20, 1990. The effect of his decision, Vincent says, means Steinbrenner's permanent banishment from baseball.

August 20, 1990: Gene Michael named vice-president and general manager. Hair color: white.

June 13, 1992: Vincent reinstates Steinbrenner to complete control of the Yankees, beginning March 1, 1993.

March 1, 1993: The Nightmare begins anew . . .

George's Faves

Favorite Color:	Blue
Favorite Car:	Limo
Favorite Food:	Ice Cream
Favorite TV Program:	The Gong Show
Favorite Musician:	John Philip Sousa
Favorite General:	Patton
Favorite Author:	Attila the Hun
Favorite Mogul (other than himself):	Trump
Favorite Commissioner:	None
Favorite Emotion:	Rage
Favorite Sport:	Football

Top Ten Really Good Things About George Steinbrenner

◆

10 Rarely breaks wind in presence of ladies

9 Always rewinds *Yankee Doodle Dandy* before returning to video store

8 Frivolous firing of employees rarely done with malice aforethought

7 Ice cream consumption keeps Hagen-Das stock strong

6 Doesn't smoke

5 Placed OTB bet for a very busy Pete Rose

4 Knows how to keep his lip buttoned

3 Upon his retirement, allowed Higgins, his loyal chauffeur, to keep his cap

2 Sold aging mother his Betamax at terrific discount

1 Reached up to top shelf in grocery store for Fay Vincent's wife

Sources

◆

Associated Press
Atlanta Constitution
Baltimore Sun
The Baseball Encyclopedia
Baseball's Greatest Quotations by Paul Dickson
The Record (Northern New Jersey)
Balls by Graig Nettles and Peter Golenbock
Boston Globe
Boston Herald
The Bronx Zoo by Sparky Lyle and Peter Golenbock
Business Week
Cable News Network
Chicago Tribune
Chicago Sun-Times
Cleveland Plain Dealer
Cleveland magazine
Dallas Morning News
Damned Yankees by Bill Madden and Moss Klein
The Economist
Esquire magazine
Gannett News Service
Hartford Courant
Houston Chronicle
Los Angeles Times
Minneapolis–St. Paul Star Tribune
National Sports Daily
Newark Star-Ledger
New York Daily News
New York Newsday
New York Post

New York Times

New York magazine

Newsweek

No Matter How Thin You Slice It, It's Still Baloney, edited by Jean Arbeiter

Number One by Billy Martin and Peter Golenbock

Oakland Tribune

The Official New York Yankees Hater's Handbook by William Mead

Orange County Register

Pinstripe Pandemonium by Geoffrey Stokes

Playboy magazine

St. Petersburg Times

San Diego Union and Tribune

Ski Racing magazine

Sport magazine

Sporting News

Sports Illustrated

Sports Wit by Lee Green

Steinbrenner! by Dick Schaap

Time magazine

USA Today

U.S. News & World Report

Wall Street Journal

Washington Post

Winfield: A Player's Life by David Winfield with Tom Parker

The Yankees by Dave Anderson, Murray Chass, Robert Creamer and Harold Rosenthal

The Yankee Quizbook by Bob Weil & Jim Fitzgerald

There's an epidemic with 27 million victims. And no visible symptoms.

It's an epidemic of people who can't read.

Believe it or not, 27 million Americans are functionally illiterate, about one adult in five.

The solution to this problem is you... when you join the fight against illiteracy. So call the Coalition for Literacy at toll-free **1-800-228-8813** and volunteer.

Volunteer Against Illiteracy. The only degree you need is a degree of caring.